Song of the Sparrow

Nihil Obstat:
    Rev Hilarion Kistner, O.F.M.
    Rev. Lawrence J. Mick

Imprimi Potest:
    Rev. Andrew Fox, O.F.M.
    Provincial

Imprimatur:
    + Daniel E. Pilarczyk, V.G.
    Archdiocese of Cincinnati
    March 16, 1976

Cover design by Robert Stevenson and Michael Reynolds
Portrait, back cover, by Mike Sipkoski
Photographs by Marne Breckensiek, O.F.M.
Book design by Michael Reynolds

SBN 0-912228-26-1

Song of the Sparrow

Meditations and Poems to Pray by.

by Murray Bodo, O.F.M.

Contents

Contents

for Naomi Burton Stone
and Roger Huser, o.f.m.

Introduction

There is something ragged and unfinished about sparrows; yet they have always endeared themselves to me. There is something Franciscan about their simplicity, their habit-colored feathers, and their availability when other birds hide away in the woods or fly south for the winter. This book is sparrow-talk, becoming song from time to time. I hope it is simple and unaffected song like the song of the sparrow.

1: Autumn

1. A Walk in the Woods

A walk in the woods. The autumn rains have turned the leaves to mulch beneath my feet and black trees are slowly emerging from their green cover of leaves. Thought-time again. In summer prayer comes with difficulty in the heavy-hanging air, but with fall as the leaves rush down, our thoughts rush heavenward again. Perhaps it is our own mortality we see in autumn leaves, perhaps it is the clearing of the skies that were blocked by green foliage. Whatever it is, fall brings with it a clearing of the mind and heart,

3

and we look up and out of ourselves for a Presence who has in his hands the life that will lie hidden till spring.

What is this prayer of fall? Mostly it rises from an emptiness caused by nature's dying into winter. And in a sense this emptiness, this longing to live, is the beginning of all prayer. I walk in the bleak November woods and I want to believe that I am not alone, that this loneliness is illusion only. And so I reach out and call upon God and I am no longer alone. For there behind the wet, behind the black trees, behind my own feelings, is He who walked the same earth and entered into its dark soil only to rise again opening forever the dark recesses of the earth and of the heart of man. And I thank him and this too is prayer.

I am sitting in a high back rocker smoking my favorite tobacco and looking at the large maple tree that fills my whole window with its leaves. And this staring becomes a part of prayer. Who can pray who does not make time for staring out windows? Prayer requires time, and time we jealously hoard for what we consider most important in our lives. Perhaps time is for recreation or work or sleep or watching T.V. I usually can tell what is really important to me by the amount of time I am willing to spend on it. And if I am willing to "waste" time on something, it is usually because I have done it before and found it worthwhile.

This previous satisfying experience is so important to any prayer-life that will endure. I must have experienced somewhere, sometime, the presence of the Lord in my life in order to long to meet him again in prayer. I must have found sitting in a rocker and smoking a pipe pleasant and relaxing if I am to return to it often. The more fulfilling the experience is, the more I will be drawn to repeat it.

Fulfillment, of course, is a tricky, loosely used word; and if I place too much emphasis on my own fulfillment, I will pray only when I foresee or experience some personal satisfaction. But if my fulfillment comes from rendering to God what is his despite my own feelings at the time, then justice and duty will prevail and I will continue prayer throughout all the seasons of my life. Fulfilling my obligations to the good God will satisfy my own need for fulfillment in the long run whereas seeking my own fulfillment will not ultimately fulfill my obligation to God or myself.

Out of the heart
The song rises,
The mind searching
for notes
to capture
its flight.

Remembering the
mountains, I sit down and dream. I see them
again the way they closed out what was ugly
beyond them. They were always forming deep
gorges and valleys where you could walk and fish,
sealed in by twelve-thousand-foot peaks that
made you feel secure and unafraid of anything
except perhaps the mountains themselves, but
that was in the winter time. And the little narrow gauge train that whistled in once a day
never seemed an intruder but a contact with a
world you wanted to be "out there" as long as
you didn't have to live in it, and it stayed a
comfortable distance away.

I have been a Francis-
can for some twenty years, and this fact makes
me think once again of the vows and their significance in the life of a friar. Unfortunately, they
sometimes amount to nothing more than a com-

mitment to "hang in there." Surely, an impoverished idea of the vows, but perhaps sufficient to get us over the rough spots. The vows, however, have to amount to a lot more than that. They should be a commitment to grow into a new man in Christ, and they should be made with this transformation into Christ as their chief motivation. I must, in making my vows, firmly believe that I am entering into the work of the Lord, that I am entering upon a long process of purification and liberation to which God has called me by name.

If my vows amount to nothing more than hanging around friaries and wearing the habit, then certainly they are a mockery of every man's fundamental call to grow in the Lord. And if after giving up everything for Christ with one side of my mouth, I then gradually call it back with the other side, the vows themselves can become little insurance policies guaranteeing a comfortable, mediocre life of non-involvement with God or my fellowman.

My potential for love and service should gradually be made real and operative by my poverty, chastity, and obedience. Otherwise, why make a vow in the first place? Unselfish love and transformation into Christ are both the motivation for and the purpose of my vows. And this love and Christ-likeness is also the measure of how well I am living my vows. I try to live my vows with God's help, and he works the transformation with my help. For no vow to the Lord is one-sided. He

promises literally everything in return for my gift,
and the Lord is faithful to his promises.

Thank you, Lord,
For your support.
Without you life is
impossible and becomes a contest
of personalities, in which the strong
and self-assured always win.
When the weak and despised and unlearned
prevail, then I know you are working
and not man's own perverse self-will.
Only your Spirit is wisdom and only
they are wise who open themselves to
that Spirit and surrender to your Father's
will. Come, Lord Jesus.

Our lives are a forgetting and a remembering. A rhythm that follows us
relentlessly till death. We are alive and doing and
we try to forget the fears and anxieties about the
future which paralyze us in the present and make
us dead and inactive. We are people who hope and
believe and so we try to remember the good the
Lord has done for us. We recall his faithfulness
and his care, and we become men of the future
who dare to act because we forget our failures and

remember God's action in our every thought and deed. We try to remember more than we forget, and we stay sane because our eyes are on him who loves us and proves it when we dare to live for him. If we remember to remember the Lord, we find our lives are meaningful and free.

The presence of God in your life. You cannot merit such an experience; and even if you are not aware of God's closeness to you but continue to do his will, he is dwelling within you. Yet, you still long to experience his presence and pray that he will reveal himself to you. Is this selfishness? I don't think it is because this longing is something beyond your control. Turn wherever you may, nothing and no one short of God can satisfy your longing or distract you from that gnawing in the mind and heart which speaks of an emptiness that is yet to be filled. Your faith says that in heaven longing will cease and every tear will be wiped away. But that future seldom suffices to make the present any less painful. And so you continue to search for God, the Living Lord.

Every man who turns to God, at one time or another asks himself if God is, or if he is deceiving himself in order to explain his own unfulfilled life. And then subtly in ways he did not expect, the Lord comes to him fleetingly to keep alive the longing and the hope of the resurrected life to come. God never comes on our own terms but in his own time and place, and his appearance is always a surprise. No one ever sees God, of course, but we see the shadows of his passing through our lives in the things that change which we never thought would, in the prayers that are answered in ways we never expected, in a new level of maturity that we know we couldn't have arrived at alone. And once again our faith is enkindled, and we begin to hope for more, for a sound in the air, for a sign unmistakable and clear.

God is a lover and he leads us artfully, attracting us, then showering us with blessings, then withdrawing to start the process all over again on a new level.

The primacy of forgiveness. Until we learn to forgive deeply and sincerely, we remain only on the threshold of real union with God, we remain essentially imprisoned and unfree. In the course of a lifetime, we gradually accumulate countless little resentments which if allowed to grow, become big hates and seemingly insoluble differences. If, however, we do not allow these jealousies and hates to grow, but instead try always to purify our hearts, we enter into the mystery of love, the mystery of God.

We have so much to forgive: life, maybe, certainly those who have hurt us, and even ourselves, perhaps most of all, ourselves. Often we are hardest on ourselves and need to forgive ourselves for failing, for being less perfect than we would like to be. God forgives us much more readily than we forgive ourselves, and that is the cause of much of our pain and inability to grow.

Forgive then, and you will begin to live. When Jesus said, "Love your enemies," it was not so much for your enemies' sake as for your own. For when you hate, you become small and petty, and the worm of decay eats at your heart, and the taste in your mouth is bitter. But when you forgive and love those who persecute you, you grow big and surpass even your own imaginings of what you could become. Love is expansive and its taste is sweet to the mouth.

Give thanks to the Lord always and your life will be a song. Some songs are sad, of course, but the melody is still there as well as the movement and the feeling of freedom that come from music. To praise and thank God, no matter what happens, is a gift which few possess. To lift your voice and heart on high in failure and defeat places you among the saints of God.

For only faith and love can explain a song of praise and thanksgiving when times are bad.

2. Trusting

Trusting the Lord. Self-confidence and confidence in God are so closely connected that we can confuse one with the other. Sometimes when I say I have lost my trust in God, I really mean I have lost confidence in myself. Or when I say I have no self-confidence, I mean I have lost my trust in the Lord's care for me. When all is going well in my life, I usually have boundless confidence in myself, and perhaps I don't even think of God.

These random thoughts raise the question of how much each person fashions for himself a God to fit his own personality. In thinking about this question and noticing how many people have a different God from mine, I suddenly realized that God himself manifests himself differently to every man. The basic revelation is constant and more or less the same for all Christians, but the God who is experienced is different because he is experienced by different personalities. God makes himself known to each man as the kind of person whom that man can love and adore. That is why a straight-laced person has a straight-laced God and a flexible person's God is understanding and tolerant.

The only assurance of some common idea of God is the Church, but even the Church does no more than insure an orthodoxy of ideas about God. The living God who is experienced is still personal in the sense that he is my God, who lives and acts in my life, and who is grasped and known by my unique personality. The God who is is universal. The God who is known by me is unique to me.

How many things have we hidden away in our memories, afraid to look at them, to bring them to the surface and kill them by facing them and seeing that they are

not so bad as we thought? And if we look at them
with Jesus at our side, it is easier still because they
are healed by his sharing the memories with us.
We are sometimes so successful in suppressing
what we do not want to remember that to our
conscious mind the experience is as if it never
happened. But it smolders beneath the surface,
burning little holes in our wills when we want to
do something and find we cannot do it. If we let
the Lord share these memories with us, they lose
all their power to scare us into inactivity. And
this healing process frees us from the past.

*O*ne of the disturbing
things about reaching middle age in the service of
the Lord, is that I sometimes feel that I know
God no better now than when I was fourteen, and
the twenty-five years or so intervening have not
been fruitful of a deepening awareness of God in
my life. I regard this sort of thinking as a temptation, mainly because I *have* persevered for all
these years. No one, I feel, can persevere in God's
service without God and without his constant
operation, without being led by the Spirit of God.

Some of the other experiences of my life are
more intense but they are sporadic and short-lived.

I do not experience God in my life the way I experience the presence of people I love, but everything I do and everything I am presupposes he dwells within me. That is perhaps sufficient for anyone, and anything beyond that is super-abundant gift.

Without charity no one will survive. Hatred destroys the hater but not before he has inflicted martyrdom on those around him. This is especially true when those hated or snubbed or made fun of are restrained from striking back by their own charitableness and willingness to forgive.

The Franciscan charism is intimately tied up with loving those who are seemingly unlovable or who return love with hatred and contempt. St. Francis, in reaching out to the leper, paved the way for his followers to walk. And like St. Francis, when we let the Lord lead us among those who are seemingly repulsive, our love makes them beautiful and they become a source of sweetness and joy to us. This is so not because we are patronizing them or "doing good" but because *we* are changed inside and begin to see people as they really are in God's sight. Our vision is cleared of our own prejudices and dimness of perception.

For only love opens our eyes to what is really there.

The tragedy of those who don't have charity is that they project their own failures and ugliness on others and think that the evil and imperfection inside is really outside them and resides in people and situations they can't stand. And that is what it means to be spiritually blind. It's hard to see anything but splinters with a beam in your own eye.

"Writing is a form of therapy; sometimes
I wonder how all those who do not
write, compose or paint can manage
to escape the madness, the melancholia,
the panic fear which is inherent in
the human condition." Graham Greene

The love of God. Who can measure its depth and breadth? Is it not one who, poor and weak, calls upon the Lord as his only support? When all else fails, and sometimes only then, do we realize we are dependent creatures who live and grow only in the Lord.

Some men long to know that truth experientially but cannot. They know they are weak and in need, but their only dependence is on what they can see and hear and feel. They want to believe that God is there: independent, all-knowing, all-loving. But they cannot make that jump, and they wonder why a God who is supposed to exist doesn't help them see, help them make that jump.

This is a great mystery. Why do some possess that inestimable gift of faith through no apparent merit of their own, and others who long for it stand empty-hearted and bereaved? The mystery lies somewhere in the center of the statement, God is love. Love does not force nor does it push us into things. Love invites, and we respond. To all appearances the jump is absurd, a risk we take that involves all kinds of human faiths that precede divine faith. We dare to believe on the word of others. We dare to believe that when we pray, we are not in fact talking to ourselves but that someone actually hears and answers. And the biggest step of all, we accept that Jesus Christ is the Incarnate Son of God, himself God and co-equal to the Father. And to top it off, these invitations to faith are often made by men who seem fanatic or at least a bit crazed by some strange illusion that they are different from other men, possessed by God himself.

Those who have been born into a family of faith find this jump fairly easy, but those whose background is non-religious find this world of faith a strange world indeed.

When God allows
sorrow and affliction to come into our lives, he
always has his own timetable. He asks us to bear
our cross for a certain period of time and nothing
we try to do seems to lift that cross from our
shoulders entirely until we are transformed and
God is ready to elevate us to a new level of love.
God is never the author of evil, but sorrow and
affliction are not necessarily evil; and if they
come from the Lord, they prove always to be for
our own good, not just in eternity but here and
now. God can, of course, bring good even out of
evil, as St. Augustine says. But what I am talking
about here are those little neuroses and disabilities
and anxieties that come into our lives and which
we try desperately to understand and rid ourselves of, sometimes for years on end. And then
one day they are no longer there and we find ourselves ready to meet life, more humble and trusting in the goodness and providence of God.

From these painful visitations of the Lord we
always grow, and we always know that they were
good for us even though we did not understand
why when they were upon us. And strangely, past
experience does not seem to make the next cross

any easier, though in some there is a positive acceptance of God's will that makes even of suffering a walking with the Lord that has its own kind of joy. In all of this those without faith often see a masochism or self-hatred that can be there but need not be. It is all in the heart and mind of the sufferer, and only God knows that.

More valuable than any logic or proof demonstrated in books is a personal experience of God. People of prayer and interiority know God mainly through his *working* in their lives. They have known the Lord in the prayers he has answered, in problems and difficulties overcome that only the power of the Spirit can explain, and above all in the charity of their lives that transcends human patience and love and reaches a level of selflessness that faith alone makes possible.

The witness of a selfless God-centered life, therefore, is the greatest proof of the existence of God. People find God in other people who have already found him and live in his love.

One of the deepest sources of joy is the awareness of healing taking place inside us. When we have been ill or depressed or confused and afraid, we pray mightily for deliverance. And one day we suddenly notice that something is happening, that our health of mind or body is returning. And this steady growth of strength and peace within us is like a new birth, a new chance to live again.

That is what happens to us in the Sacrament of Penance. Our sins are forgiven as soon as we confess them and are absolved, but the healing is a gradual process. Gradually and imperceptibly we are being made whole, and then one day we realize that **something** wonderful has happened to us. What before seemed impossible is now possible and what was previously so difficult is now somehow easy.

Most healing of the spirit is effected only when we verbalize our hurt, when we say to another that we have sinned or that we are troubled deep inside. The Sacrament of Penance provides that kind of therapy. And it gives us the opportunity to listen as well. We listen to the word of God and to the words of the priest and we pray with him

21

for healing. Everyone needs healing, and to neglect an opportunity like the Sacrament of Penance is to let pass one of the most effective ways in which we grow from inner sickness to health.

I lean on God, but from time to time I feel that I am leaning on air alone. That happens when I start putting God out there somewhere too far removed from me. When I remember that he dwells in me and in all my brothers and sisters in Christ, then that leaning becomes substantial again and God takes flesh in those around me whom I can see and hear. We are the body of Christ, and he has no other visible body here and now. God is spirit but he has become enfleshed in Jesus and Jesus takes on flesh and bone in us through the same Holy Spirit. When we lean on one another then, we are building up the Body of Christ. We are strengthening our own weakness by acknowledging that we are only a part of the whole Body and that we need all the other members if we are going to function correctly and appreciate our own worth. By leaning, we stand upright and God becomes real for us because we are no longer trying to be our own strength. Christ marrows in us.

*D*o we make order
with words? Do we find, as Robert Frost says,
some momentary stay against confusion in the
well-made poem? In the making of a poem, in the
doing, there is the order that comes from the
discipline imposed by words. Words, properly
arranged, are the essence of our thinking. When
we are confused, our words are confused. And if
we cannot sort out our own confusion, we can at
least try to impose order upon words on the page.
In ordering these words, perhaps my own thinking will become clear or at least clearer than it was
before I put them down. As E. M. Forster once
wrote, "How do I know what I think until I see
what I say?"

I know that the love of
God must have the first place in my life. And
when I let it slip behind any other love, there is
tension and confusion in my heart. All other loves,
if they are not second to the love of God, become

stumbling blocks to my own growth and inner freedom. If I am to be free, then God alone has first claim on my heart. My time and preoccupation must be with doing his will, with pleasing him. This lesson is learned daily, and each new love is a challenge to this simple truth: All loves are purified in the love of him who made love.

*T*he most important secret of the life of prayer is that we must learn to pray without a sideward glance to see if anyone is watching. We must go into our room, close the door, and pray to our Father in secret. This entering into our room and closing the door is something we must do even when we are praying in public, even when we are praying with others, and maybe especially then. Otherwise like King Claudius in Shakespeare's, *Hamlet,* we cry out, "My words fly up, my thoughts remain below. / Words without thoughts never to Heaven go."

If our words are calculated to please others or to impress them, or if we use our prayer to bolster our own egos before others, then our thoughts remain below. Our concentration must be on God, who lifts us up and out of ourselves. If our thoughts during prayer are truly on God, then we will be accepted and admired by others. For then, and only then, will we be independent enough of our fellows and dependent enough on God to be truly ourselves. And when we are truly ourselves, we are lovable enough to be loved.

Sometimes I cannot sleep at night because the Lord is stirring my soul. I have no direct experience of him, but my restlessness and tossing makes me rise and take pen in hand to record my own weakness and his great love and kindness. Praise him who acts in our lives when we think it is only our nerves or our inability to unwind and let nature take its course. When we rise and do his will, we sleep well the remainder of that time we call the night.

The love of God. How little is it understood or believed. So many people do not believe that they are loved or loveable. And yet God sent his only Son to die for each one of us in an unbelievable act of love. Perhaps that "unbelievable" is why many can't believe. Maybe it is incredible that we could be so wonderful in God's eyes that he would go this far to impress upon us our own worth. But if we can accept the fact of this love of God for us, we regain our self-respect and dignity and walk free as sons of God.

I have a Father who loves me, a Brother who died for me, and a Spirit within me who is the pledge and proof of their love. In that very Spirit I have the power to talk to the Father and the Son and know that they hear me, for I speak in the Spirit who is himself God and inseparable from the Father and the Son. This is the beginning, middle, and end of all prayer.

Someone once told me he had taken up sky-diving because he had no reason for not doing it except that he was afraid, and he did not want to start not doing things simply because he was afraid. How much good is left undone and how many dreams and hopes are shattered for lack of courage. Fear can steal into our lives so subtly that we might not even recognize it at first. We may think it prudence at first, or good sense. But ultimately it shows its ugly head for what it is, a killer and paralyzer of action and the fulfillment that comes from doing.

*T*o slow down and let the healing happen. How hard that is when the very sickness is a fear of slowing down, of not being able to function as well as we could, of paralysis of will. Healing is most impossible when we cannot forget the sickness long enough for healing to start.

*P*ractically every Christian book on prayer is simply a commentary on the Lord's Prayer. Jesus' own formula for prayer is *the* model of how we should pray. All true prayer should take us out of ourselves, out of the narrow confines of our self-conscious preoccupation with our own thoughts and feelings. Jesus' prayer does that immediately: "Our Father who art in heaven." We are out of ourselves, addressing our Father, calling upon God himself as our Father. And this other-centeredness continues: "hallowed be thy Name." God's name defines who he is, is synonymous with who he is. And we pray that his name always be Holy. Reverence, respect, adoration of whom we are daring to address. "Thy Kingdom come." Praying for God's Kingdom to come is saying yes to all of salvation history and yes for all that is yet to come in the plan of God. And then perhaps the hardest prayer of all: "Thy Will be done." God's Will! To say yes to that is to accept the totality of what has happened, is happening, and will yet come to pass as it is willed by the Father. And that means suffering and sorrow as well as happiness and joy. This whole first part of the Lord's Prayer has been addressed to the Father and has been wishing for him everything he wants from man: That he be our Father, that his Name be holy, that his kingdom come, and his will be done. And we pray for all of this not to *My* Father, but to *Our* Father because we are one with all mankind whose common Father is our personal Father as well.

Only then do we pray for ourselves and all mankind. "Give us this day our daily bread." We trust in our Father's loving providence to care for us from day to day. We live and pray in the present and God answers our present needs, not those future needs we imagine are coming. "And forgive us our trespasses as we forgive those who trespass against us." No prayer is possible without forgiveness. We must forgive those who offend us if we are to expect God to forgive us our offenses. A heart that cannot forgive is a closed heart and God will not enter there. "And lead us not into temptation, but deliver us from evil." We acknowledge our fallen nature and our dependence on God. Only in him can we be victorious over evil, and only a humble awareness of our need for him will keep us from succumbing to temptation. For his is the Kingdom and the power and the glory for ever. As we began with praise, we end with praise; and everything in between flows from that praise. Very simply, that is what prayer is all about.

*I*n fall the trees turn and the skies clear and I remember New Mexico. One of the most enduring of my childhood memories is the bright blue of New Mexico's skies. Even the memory of that blue clears my mind. I don't remember the trees turning when I was a boy, but their turning now is a signal that a little bit of New Mexico will be transported here to Ohio: the leaves will fall and I will see the sky again. On a clear day I am renewed as I am at other times only when I am on the beach listening to the sea sing.

29

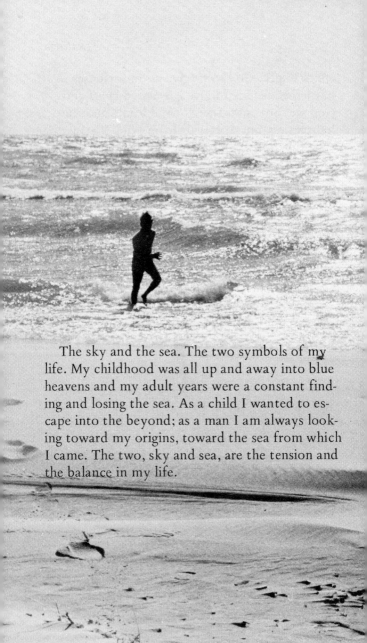

The sky and the sea. The two symbols of my life. My childhood was all up and away into blue heavens and my adult years were a constant finding and losing the sea. As a child I wanted to escape into the beyond; as a man I am always looking toward my origins, toward the sea from which I came. The two, sky and sea, are the tension and the balance in my life.

*T*rue love is relatively free of emotional dependence on the beloved. And this includes the love of God.

3. Signs of His Presence

Jeremiah. Always before me, prophet who speak personally to my heart. You, Jeremiah, in your vocation, make my own vocation real. Your vocation is the prototype of every vocation. Without you, I would give up and say it is foolish to serve God this way. But because of you I know I was called before I was born, that God cares enough to send even you, even me, to be his mouth, his broken body, his crippled mind. And men listen because God speaks through the most improbable of men. Those who are too obviously God's instruments last only for their own lifetimes because they are their own mouthpieces and the message dies when they do. They who speak for God live forever in God's word, which outlives the instrument of its speaking.

*T*he healing power of God. Rarely do we realize the healing that is going on inside us. We do not notice it, because we mistake it for something else, we mistake it for evil. If we have learned to enter into prayer, then we see with new eyes and hear with new ears. And what we perceive is that what we previously thought was surely some scourge of Satan in our lives, is in fact the healing hand of God leading through the fire of suffering in order to purify and heal what only suffering *can* heal.

We never love the suffering, and it is not lessened by our new consciousness, but our *faith* is strengthened because we begin to see connections and patterns in our lives. We see that each new pain, each new difficulty leads us to a new level of maturity and healthy dependence on the God who loves us. Why this growth must come through suffering is a mystery, but we know that the mystery is somehow inseparably linked with the cross of Christ. Only one who has accepted the reality of that cross and its redemptive power can ever

accept the fact that suffering is growth, that
paralysis is movement on another level. Only in
the mystery of the cross are T. S. Eliot's lines
intelligible: "Suffering is action and action is
suffering."

Poetry works too power-
fully on me to submit myself lightly to any poet.
It is like friendship. I have to trust before I love.
Most people I know start with love. I love poetry
as an abstraction, but individual poems grow on
me as I learn to trust the poet through his poem.
For the poem is the poet and what is said is who
is saying it. Some sayings are unreliable. I look
for the transcendent in the particular. Particulars
in themselves tend to be self-serving and convo-
luted. Only the transcendent, the metaphysical,
frees the particular concrete experience from the
poet's own introversion.

The real signs of our
faith are often the men and women we know.
Some are evident signs of faith, hope, and char-

ity, and others signs of contradiction. It is the latter people who disturb us and make us question whether we are seeing things aright. Those who are hostile and aggressive and who speak like Old Testament prophets, make us wonder if they are real. The meek and humble somehow beguile us by their gentleness and littleness.

Trying to write something everyday is like trying to pray everyday: You have to discipline yourself to it because there are always more "important" things or more fun things to do. But if you steel yourself to setting time aside, things begin to happen while you are in the process of writing or praying. Flannery O'Connor once said, "Every morning between 9 and 12 I go to my room and sit before a piece of paper. Many times I just sit for three hours with no ideas coming to me. But I know one thing: If an idea does come between 9 and 12, I am there ready for it." That quote is one of the most perfect descriptions of what happens in prayer that I have ever seen.

For me prayer and writing often go together. But even if they don't for someone else, the process of the two is much the same. I must be willing to sit before a blank piece of paper, as it were, if I am ever going to learn to pray. Time for staring and time for waiting. Patience to wait for God to act, for God to speak. If I expect something tangible to happen inside me every time I pray, then my prayer has become superstition or magic. All I have to do is utter certain formulae and God appears like some genie. If this were the case, God would not be God, but some puppet of man. And God *is* the Lord, he *is* God.

Therefore, I make myself available to him and I pray. He will come when he will come if I persevere in prayer just as the idea comes and "happens" on the paper if I persevere in writing. Inspiration comes while I am in the process of putting words on paper, and God comes while I am involved in that process called prayer.

What is a Franciscan? No mold here. No simple answer. St. Francis himself was so much out of the mold, so much a charismatic figure, that to expect a uniformity of life-style among his followers is to presume some kind of monastic superimposition on a movement which is essentially non-monastic. The Franciscan life is the gospel life, lived purely and simply, with the one reservation that it is totally and unreservedly submissive to the "Roman Church," as St. Francis himself put it. Most friars I know are signs of contradiction. They are very much free spirits, and yet they are held in a mysterious magnetic field which is their fraternity, their dependence upon their brothers in St. Francis. We are brothers to one another, and in all our eccentricities, we seem never to forget this.

We are, besides, sons of the Church, ever mindful of St. Francis' words, "Brother Francis promises obedience and reverence to his holiness Pope Honorius and his lawfully elected successors and to the Church of Rome." Only such obedience and reverence can explain how so much diversity as the Friars personify could have survived these some 750 years.

The Franciscan vocation is essentially charismatic and Jesus-oriented and only obedience and reverence for the Holy See can keep such enthusiasm sane. Francis knew that and so do his true followers. They look always to the Bishop of Rome. And in the earth-shaking transition that is taking place secularly and religiously in the mid-twentieth century, Francis' admonition to be obedient to Rome is one of the few stabilities left. Everyone needs guidance from others from time to time, but no one so much as a liberated man like a follower of Francis of Assisi. Living the gospel is so treacherous that, unguided, it has led to some of the most atrocious crimes and aberrations in history. A proud enthusiast can justify just about anything from coercion to Baptism to the genocide of all Jews, all in the name of Jesus. The followers of St. Francis have been spared that kind of fanaticism by Francis' simple command that they remember they are not the Church of God, but remain submissive to that Church, whether that means the Hierarchical Church or the People of God.

Individual friars have erred, to be sure, but the fraternity itself has in the main been sensible enough to survive over 750 years, and yet continue to inspire the most diverse of men to leave everything and follow the Little Poor Man of Assisi. Their charism from Francis and their obedience to the Holy Father have made that balance possible. For charism is purified in obedience as Jesus' life amply exemplifies. "Not my will but thine be done." And, "I come to do the will of my Father." And, "I do the will of him who sent me." There is always someone whose will I acknowledge and from whom my charism comes. The Franciscan is anointed by the Spirit and purified and directed by that same Spirit's Church.

I write even when I am
tired. It reminds me to pray even when I'm tired.
With both writing and prayer there is something
to show afterwards. Not much usually, but
enough to make you glad you did it, if only because God is your witness.

Perhaps this is an insight;
perhaps not. Most books about monasticism stress
that one enters the monastery to find God. The
Franciscan experience seems to me to be different: Having had an experience of God, I join the
Franciscan Brotherhood to live out that experience in its fullest implications and to do penance
for my sins which knowing God has made me
conscious of. This does not mean that the Franciscan has found his God and that the monk is
searching for his. That would be absurd. No one
ever "finds" God in this life, and every man is
searching for him from saint to sinner. But the
Franciscan approach to life in the spirit is different from that of the monk. The Friar's life is
more service than search as the monk's life leans
more to search than service. Both, of course,
serve and both search. But the emphasis is differ-

ent. Both feel the tension between serving and searching, and both find some middle ground where they can live the Gospel life while searching for what that Gospel is.

God spoke to Francis and he went out to rebuild the Church; the monk starts working in the fields and God speaks to him.

This, however, is only the beginning. The friar soon finds out that his first experience of God is somehow lost in his task of rebuilding the Church, and he must constantly turn to prayer to try and recapture his first vision. In the process a new vision unfolds and a "new" God is revealed to him. And the friar, too, ends up searching in prayer for his God.

The monk who hears God is tempted to leave off working in the fields in order to deepen his experience of God, but he soon discovers that the pursuit of God without the therapy of work leads to madness, and he returns to the fields in search of the voice that spoke to him in the sweat of his brow. Too much work or too much prayer leads to imbalance in the interior life, and in the search for that balance the apostle and the contemplative merge into every man.

4. Freeing the Spirit

The trouble with selfishness and greed is that it slips so easily from material things to things of the spirit like reputation, or honor, or appreciation, and fame. And this need to hold on to adulation slips sooner or later into a kind of slavery to other people's opinion of us. This whole process turns us increasingly inward; and ironically, it makes us insecure and fearful. So that what began as an ego-building enterprise like building the Tower of Babel, ends in confusion of tongue and heart and I am frightened to say what I mean or to mean what I say.

On the other hand, selflessness and material generosity flow from and into spiritual freedom.

And this free spirit leads me unerringly out of my-self to him who is perfect freedom and in whom and for whom I move with the uninhibited free-dom of a child. I become existentially aware that I am a child of a God who loves me like a Father, and everything I do becomes a gift for him, to please him and thank him for being who he is to me. Gradually, the negativism and disapproval of life's persistent critics means little at all when compared to my determination to do the will of him who made me and redeemed me. Even my occasional ignorance of what that will is, is puri-fied in my intention to do it as best I can.

What I admire most in a piece of writing is the feeling that I am read-ing something said well, that I am reading some-one who has something to say and who has mas-tered the craft of putting his ideas down on paper so that they stick in the mind. This craft does not come easy. And as I try to stumble through my own writing, I grow daily in my admiration for what goes into the making of a great work of literature. At times the making seems more impor-tant to me than the "finished" work itself.

The same holds true when I meet someone who

is genuinely holy. I say, "My God, the self-sacrifice and surrender to God's will that must have gone into all this person is!" And where the person has come from and the journey getting to this point become more important than what he is. This is especially true for people because unlike works of art, they are never really finished; they are ever in the process of growing or regressing. And holiness means that they are growing more than they are regressing; and though growth is the nature of all living things, growth in selfless love is not natural to fallen man. Only the power of God's Spirit and man's surrender to it can explain a steady growth in charity. That process is more wonderful than any other creating I know of. The greatest art is the art of entering into that death and resurrection cycle we call redemptive love.

*T*o love God with our whole heart and our whole soul and our whole mind. What does that mean? Does it mean, for example, that there is no love left for anyone other than God? Such a love would be absurd for a human being. And what is inhuman is surely not Divine. My love for God must be whole-hearted and he must come first, but in him and because

of him all my other loves are purified and actually
made possible. The more I love God, the more human I become, for I am made in his image. My
humanity mirrors him who made me. If on the
other hand, my love is primarily for the Church or
my work or someone other than God, I begin to
lose my humanness, for I have set up an idol in
the place of my Creator, and I begin to resemble
the idol. My humanity is tied closely to divinity,
for to be human is to be like God in whose image
I am created. The more God-like I am, the more
I am myself. But the more myself I am does not
necessarily mean the more God-like I am. For
often in striving to be myself, I can be setting up
another idol, namely a false image of who I think
I am. I find myself in God, but I do not necessarily find God in myself. The self cultivated can
end up being the most pernicious of all idols. But
the cultivation of the love of God invariably leads
to the greatest possession of myself.

I haven't written for a
week or so. Too many distractions, too much
work to do. Funny, I haven't prayed as much
either. God's subtle reminder that I have to make
time for him and myself.

When I compare my-
self with others, I have an immense sense of
failure, of inadequacy because I see only their
strengths which seldom are my strengths. But
when I forget comparisons and look only to what
needs to be done, what can be done, I am at peace
in the knowledge that I have something to give,
something to offer. If I give of myself, it will
make a difference, even though someone else
could have given more, could have loved more
perfectly, could have succeeded where I failed. If
only everyone realized that the gift he can give is
unique and does make a difference! What pain of
self-pity he would be spared! We can never be the
people we admire. We can only be ourselves, and
that alone is admirable.

May my gift be
acceptable to you, O Lord, for it is all I have to
give. May my gift be acceptable to you, O man,
for it is the same gift I offer to God: myself, my
love.

In the night
Alone with my thoughts
I remember you, O God;
And my empty room
And emptier thoughts
Are filled with your
Love, your watchful care.
And loneliness is changed
To praise, to gratitude
That empty hearts
Are lodges for your
Loving presence.

Why is it so hard to talk about God or write about him without sounding general and full of platitude and cliche? Isn't it because our experience of God is so personal that to talk about his love sounds like self-celebration, sounds as if we are making ourselves special souls upon whom God has lavished his love? Or is it because we really don't know if God is present to us in a personal way and so we repeat what Scripture says God is supposed to do? For my own part, my book on God would be my own autobiography, because I don't know God apart from what he has done for me, through me, with me, and in me, and in all those I've known in my life.

I confess my small insecurities, O Lord, because of the one big security of you.

I wonder at times why I keep a notebook. What secret compulsion makes me put pen to paper day after day? And always I hear in my heart some intangible voice that says someone may find you, O Lord, in an entry that I took time to write down. It is that way with all our acts, really. In you they somehow have a deeper, more lasting significance than our mere doing them would seem to warrant. And your words about the cup of water offered to the very least of your brothers echo in my mind. Nothing is ever lost on you, Lord. You grace all our goings and all our smallest touches of love with your redemptive power. We sanctify everything we touch and, sadly, we seldom know we are redeeming and deifying creation by a mere smile. All of this once seemed sentimental to me, but then I suppose we do move from our spiritual adolescence into the childhood of maturity.

The most relevant writer I've
ever read is William Shakespeare,
And he mostly wrote about the past.

*W*e re-learn the lesson
of detachment with each new straw we clutch at
in the wind. Funny thing about straw in the wind:
we never forget that it is only straw, but when
nothing else is left to cling to, straw suddenly has
all the attraction and beauty of a messenger sent
from God to give us new life and love. And so,
deceived again, we reach out and try to build
something solid with straw. And it dries up and
blows away before our eyes, and we learn to wait
for him who sends the wind and the straw to see
if we are ready yet for him. Our reaching out for
any straw says that we are. And he comes the
minute we let the straw go without regret and
with remorse for thinking God would be content
with our choosing something less than his love.

Contrition always comes to me when I realize
How hard I've been trying to avoid living with
So elusive a lover as God. It brings with it a
Wry sense of how hard it is to live without God, as
Difficult as he is most of the time. And something
   deeper

In me makes me smile and say to myself that he is
  worth it.

Morning breaks each time you come, O Lord.
And the night picks up the shattered pieces of
  dawn
And glues them together whenever you go away.
I live in a vase broken and glued so many times
It has its own sentimental value for me.
And inside the darkness of vase I see so many
  cracks
That each new breaking is easier. Even I can do
  it now.
You used to have to break it from the outside.

Some people say if you wait for God, nothing
  will happen.
I don't believe that. A lot happens that you don't
  want to happen,
And so you say nothing has happened when you
  mean, nothing you wanted to happen came to
  pass. Surrender to what God is working within
  you, and everything that happens shines with
  your own unique light.

I write easiest at night when everyone else is
  asleep.
I pay for it dearly in the morning when everyone
  else is awake.

I write little poetry now because I haven't much time for staring out windows or walking through the woods. And prose is so much easier to write, at least for me. The self-discipline, concentration, and observation necessary for poetry are ironically luxuries in my life instead of the necessary stuff of a friar's life that they should be.

To persevere in anything is no mean achievement, because if you persevere to the end, you have persevered from day to day. If you are faithful in the end, you were faithful all along the way. It seems to me that nothing is ever achieved without a certain daily doggedness that comes from a conviction about what you are working for. Nowhere is this more evident than in prayer, for the daily fruit of prayer is at best a vague sense of peace, but more often than not, is merely a sense of having tried. However, from time to time there is a breakthrough to God that is worth the daily drudgery and is, I think, only possible because of the daily perseverance that preceded it. Not that you merit a breakthrough because you persevered, but a certain attitude of receptiveness and patience, of humility and longing grows imperceptibly but surely in the heart of anyone who prays regularly in season and out. And the cumulative experience of the prayerful man reinforces his conviction that prayer, after all, *is* communion with the God he cannot see, so that in the end he is secure in having known the Lord. He may not be able to put his finger on any one experience of God, but he will tell you that he has found God in prayer, in his life-long endeavor to pray.

> Walking the leaves down
> On an autumn afternoon
> I feel it again, that brown
> Mulching of the spirit, and
> I sense a settling in
> For winter, a searching
> For caves and nests in
> Cozy corners of my heart.

Witnessing a young
friar make his vows, I thrill at what he is doing. I
look back on my own years vowed to the Lord,
and I know something of what he will endure and
the joys he will have. Everything he experiences
from now on will either be a fulfillment of or a
challenge to St. Francis' motto, "My God and my
all." Discovering what those words mean experientially will be the warp and woof of the pattern
his own life will reveal in the end.

Each friar discovers for himself what that "all"
means. And every false god that creeps into his
life will evoke a response from God, who, when
the friar least expects, will lead him gently or not
so gently out into the desert of purification to
remind him that he is in fact a pilgrim, a wanderer,
nomadic and bent upon a heavenly city.

I sit and listen for your voice, O Lord,
And the silence of the trees is what I hear.
I look for your reflection in the lake
And I see white clouds mirrored there.
I reach out for you and feel the air.
And then I remember you are Spirit
And my own spirit breathes you in.

On the feast of St. Francis this year,
October 4, 1974, Anne Sexton was found
dead at the wheel of her car,
The engine running mechanically well.

The days of my youth
somehow are more vivid in my memory than
those of the immediate past. So much so that I
often feel like the young boy I was. Perhaps this
is more than memory. Perhaps we are always
aware of our growing, of our moving toward
something rather than having arrived. To the child
the adult seems to have arrived somewhere; to the
adult the child seems a mirror of himself.

This kind of experience in me may only reveal
that I have not really grown up yet, or it may
mean that my awareness of myself is only as
strong as my most vivid memory of myself when
I was most impressionable.

We drift away from God so easily; not fast, but easily. And before we know it, we are far down stream from him trying desperately to break our acceleration and reverse our direction. The water is always too fast at that very point, and God himself draws us back with his strong hand; that is, if we're trying to row with him.

How good is the Lord. He surprises us with his help and his love when we least expect it, and he makes it all good again—the suffering and pain, the loneliness and fear, the helplessness and despair. And when he comes, we forget the way it was without him, so compelling is the power of his presence. Nor do we fear his leaving, for when he is with us, only he occupies our mind. We rejoice because the Bridegroom is with us.

But he does leave us, or so we believe, and in the darkness it is hard to remember the light. If, however, we begin to see this pattern of the Lord's coming and going, of darkness and light in our lives, then we acquire a peace and tranquility of heart. We gradually learn that nothing in this life is forever. And with this insight we acquire the wisdom neither to despair when the Lord withdraws nor to presume that his felt presence will remain when he draws near.

What remains is the pattern of coming and going and that in itself is proof of God's presence in our lives. That movement of the Spirit of God is like the wind: it blows where and when it will and no magic of man can conjure it up nor make it disappear. And that is proof enough that the Lord *is* Lord, that he is independent of man. His love alone moves him to come to us and then only when we want him to come.

Good writing never happens when the mind is bright and clear, and the heart is warm and satisfied. It comes about when the mind is darkening and the shivering heart longs for something more or something other. Then the writer begins, and in the magic of words seeking each other and rubbing their surfaces gently, a warmth emerges until, striking each other sharply, a flame is struck from their surfaces, revealing some hidden fire within. No one knew it was there, not even the writer himself. He merely brought the words together, trying different combinations and discarding those

soft words that haven't enough flint for sparking.
If he is lucky enough to strike a fire, his mind is
lighted and his heart is warmed, and others join
him at the fire. And there around that fire civili-
zation continues.

I don't write a book; I
fill one page of a yellow legal-sized pad each day.
Neither do I achieve sanctity; I just try to do
God's will each day. In both cases what happens
eventually depends on whether or not I remember to work at it every day. If I do, God will sup-
ply the rest.

5. Rainfall and Night Thoughts

The way the rain hit my window this evening and that sudden opening of clouds awakened something inside me, and I was back in Assisi on a rainy afternoon. The same fullness was there inside me, and I was reaching for a remembered experience so satisfying that even in memory it was good. From time to time something in the landscape or the weather leaps out at us, and we feel that we have been here before, that time is being somehow reversed; and even if we don't remember what the past experience was, we re-live the feel of it.

I sometimes think heaven will be that way. It will be a new experience, but something about it will awaken that feeling that somewhere in another life we have experienced something like this newness. And it will be good, both in itself and in the remembering. For surely we are increasing our enjoyment of heaven even now. In cooperating with God here and now we are in a sense preparing part of our own heaven. In heaven there are many mansions, but we move into those mansions with our own experiences, and the fuller, the more perfect those experiences are, the greater will be our capacity to be filled with God, who though infinitely beyond our experience, will not destroy our memories of meeting him on earth.

The quiet of the night. Sometimes, sleepless, we listen to the sounds of night and count the hours with cigarettes and all-night radio shows. Perhaps we should turn off the radio, put out our cigarettes, and listen to the sound of our own hearts beating faster than they should, and in the quiet of the surrounding night, lift our minds and hearts to God whose calm heart paces the universe.

That sounds so good on paper; but whenever I

try it, it fails to produce either sleep or rest. And so I count on sleepless nights from time to time as part of the human condition. And I remember Jesus spending whole nights in prayer and try to imagine him, like me, a man with a man's problems and a man's fears. Then sleepless nights don't seem so bad, and they are even peopled with hundreds of others who cannot sleep. And strangely I sleep much better just knowing that, for what often kept me awake was the thought that everyone else was asleep.

*L*ife is full of ambiguities and unanswered questions. Yet we survive, we continue to find pleasure and joy in the smallest things. We struggle with some temptation, some problem that plagues us and makes our days heavy and our nights broken and troubled. And then for a few minutes or an hour some small surprise (a piece of music, a card game, a visit from an old friend, a scent of roses in the air), and we are temporarily drawn out of ourselves into something other.

Life should have its little surprises. When there are no more little joys, no more surprises, our own pseudo-sophistication is killing the life within us: and it is time to become like little children again. The ambiguities and questions will be there no matter what we do. The little surprises will be there only if we want them, only if we expect them to come, and that is hope. And that sustains us.

*O*ur peace comes only by doing God's will. But most of the time that will comes through other men. The great secret is to somehow know when men are speaking for God and when they are speaking only for themselves. And who knows that?

So once again obedience is the safer route; discernment is the risky one. My own preference is for obedience because I can't find anywhere in history one who was his own discerner. At least not in the Catholic tradition, and that is where I am and want to be. "Safe" then becomes realistic; "risky" ends up self-serving. I'm only talking about discerning God's will. Other cases might be different, and probably are.

*T*he one constant: God is love and faithfulness. Until we realize that God really does care, we are without faith. No assent to truths or dogmas ever substitutes for a deep, personal conviction that God loves me and cares about what happens to me. If I have all knowledge, as St. Paul says, and have not charity, what difference does it make? And charity as St. John says, is this: That God first loved us and sent his Son to redeem us. St. John complements St. Paul and tempers a lot of things that the Apostle of the Gentiles says. The King James version of the Bible puts it all together when it reads, "Believe on the Lord Jesus." Yes, only if we believe on him, does dogma and Church and sacrament and all the rest make sense. For from Jesus comes the Church and what it teaches and what it symbolizes in outward signs. Never does faith begin with something other than God himself. God initiates and everything else follows from that. And God did initiate the Church through his Son, Jesus, and from that Church everything else derives. To love the Church is to love Jesus and to love Jesus is to love God, for he is the en-fleshment of God himself.

In the end then, God's love and faithfulness is revealed once and for all in his Son, Jesus. And the love of Jesus manifest on this earth and continued after his resurrection in his followers, is the greatest proof of all that God does love and that he is faithful now — in the past — and presumably in the future, as well. If I know that God cares now through his Son, I believe he cared in the past, too, and I hope that he will care in the future. All the evidence says he will be constant; for the past and the present, when they are consistent, are pretty much infallible, as far as we know now, in predicting the future.

6. Joy in the Lord

How good is the Lord!
Whether his hand lies lightly or heavily upon us,
it is his goodness that moves him to touch us. And
we know him by this touch, this action in our
lives. Something happens which we do not expect,
and we find ourselves growing in a way we didn't
think possible or didn't even imagine existed. And
we know that God has touched us again.

*T*he Franciscan spirit.
I am always amazed at the influence the Franciscans I know have had on people. There is something of St. Francis in all of his followers. No Franciscan friar I have ever met has come out of a mold, and yet they all share something in common. What that is I really don't know. But I detect it somewhere in their approachability, their familiarity, their ease of manner. And when these qualities are missing, there is depth, a spirit of love and devotion that transcends what is merely human. I know that must sound wholly idealistic and unreal, and perhaps it is. I am so prejudiced toward the Franciscan vision of life that I automatically favor anyone who follows the Poverello of Assisi.

And perhaps that is not really bad. How great a gift it is to love something and someone so much that your whole vision of reality is colored by that vision. Isn't it more healthy to be prejudiced in others' favor rather than to be skeptical and reserved? I don't know. I only know that I feel so good when I meet another friar. Here is someone I am predisposed to love. He, too, has lain down his life for the ideals God himself gave to his ser-

vant, Francis. (Whether he really lives those ideals
only God knows.) What I know is that he has
professed the same ideals that I professed. And
how wonderful that is! I have known friars in
America and Canada and Mexico and England
and Europe, and we are all brothers — immediately upon meeting one another. Francis lives!

I pen these words in enthusiasm! I can't write
of Franciscans coldly and rationally, and I really
don't want to. I am prejudiced to the core. And
it really doesn't bother me. If it is an illusion,
don't disillusion me. If it is not, it is more wonderful than anything I know.

The providence of God!
He cares. And more, he is faithful to his word. All
of this sounds so cliche-ish, and I suppose it is,
but everyone can fill in the specifics for himself.

Always it is the
same: You suddenly realize that God has been

there all along, that yes, he is present in your life. And the words of praise and thanksgiving rise to your lips, perhaps after great sorrow or suffering or that darkness of mind which seems endless and terrible when it is upon you.

And what is it that brings that realization of God's all-loving presence? Isn't it that something changes inside you that cannot be explained by anything you did or anyone else did to you or for you? Often something you have been hoping for or praying for just happens. Perhaps you wake up one morning and something is different. You accept what you couldn't before, or you look in the mirror and laugh at yourself. And peace seeps through your whole being, and everything seems good again in spite of pain or sorrow or loss.

Joy in the Lord is not easily won, if it can be said to be won at all. Joy is a gift from God, one of his surprises that come to us when we are expecting something else. And yet I think we can also say that joy is won. It is won by those with heart enough to surrender to the Lord. God himself gives us the power to surrender, but we alone can choose to use that power. So in that sense we win our joy in the Lord. And "win" is a good word here, for the surrender is never made without a battle; and in this case by losing that battle and surrendering finally to God, we win! Another paradox, another reality that only the Spirit of God can explain. Only in the power of God's Spirit is our defeat our victory and our surrender our real possession.

The man who relies wholly on the Lord is indeed a rarity. For each one of us has his crutches, his little securities to sustain him day by day.

> Alone on a wintry night
> When the wind ticks
> Against my window
> Like nature's clock
> Reminding me of time again.

Who knows what love is? And how many who really know ever say?

Most of the love I have known has been non-verbal. It has been there in devotion and duty and fidelity. It has endured when words have failed. It has sustained me when no one knew what to say. And always behind all love has been Love himself, Jahweh, Lord, the God of all. I've never seen him or heard him. Nor have I known him as the saints and mystics have. But through it all I know he is here with me. And that is love, and all I know about it.

Others, I am aware, experience the presence of God as surely as they see and hear me. And from that deep faith they put to shame men like me who walk mostly in darkness, envying those whose Lord lives experientially within them. What keeps me going and always will is that I pray for that kind of faith. I want it and would trade anything for it. That, too, I hope is love. For if it is not, then there is no room in heaven for those who search and cry out in the night for the smallest light to see by.

O Lord, listen to me your poorest of lovers.
I come to you, as I always do, begging.
I am not ashamed to beg from you, Lord,
For you are the source of everything I have.
I see people starving and dying everywhere,
And that is what makes me ashamed to put
My poor petition before you.
Help them first, Lord. My suit can wait.

When they are satisfied, I will ask you to turn
To me. In the meantime, remember my
Frailty, Lord. Being more filled than
They, I am more vulnerable to temptation,
More apt to turn elsewhere for what you
Alone can give me. And I'll remember
Always that you are big enough to pay
Attention to us all: The famished of body
And the famished of spirit, as well.

Take me in hand, O Lord.
Though your palm be rough,
I will not shrink if only you
Man-handle me before I
Seek smoother palms and
Softer touches than yours.
I've known your firm grip
And your blows and they are
Touches of love more sure
Than any caress or soothing
Stroke of lover's tenderness.
And always it is you who man
Me again when my own
Soft heart unmakes your
Strengthening virility.

When the heart rebels and says, "I will reach out for love wherever it may be found," and the mind echoes, "Yes, and I will not see," and the conscience says, "I don't care anymore," then memory rises like a bright and redeeming sun and says, "Yes, but you have been here before and the Lord saved you in the nick of time. The Lord comes himself if you ask just one more time. Remember?" And again it is memory that cries aloud, "The Lord is faithful and he will not abandon those who trust in him." And the past is made present through memory's alchemy. This saves us time and again, and we praise and thank God who gives us the past to make the present a wise and redemptive future.

God is. Two words that make all the difference. God loves. Two words that make that difference a blessing full of joy and hope. God became man. Three words

that sum up being and loving. Being and loving
are always Trinitarian. They involve begetting
someone to prove they are real. Father and Spirit
send the Son, as Father and Son send the Spirit.
God becomes man but we don't know it until
Father and Son become Spirit within us. And Son
and Spirit within us cry out, Abba, Father, and
we know God is Father.

*I*n Italy the skies are
clearer, the lakes bluer, and the people, well, only
those who have been there know their special
resiliency. The Italian peasant is that epitome of
balance and wisdom that only soil can impart.
I've never been to Russia, but I'm sure the Rus-
sian peasant has much the same qualities as the
Italian, give or take a lot of sun or the lack of it.
In Germany and France and yes, all the rest, it
must be the same: soil and sun and clear skies,
and those who work in dirt possess that soil and
all the earth as well. And in that possession, they
become resolute and strong and stand up among
all the men of earth and smile and laugh at ideas
and cares that transcend the solid earth. And very
few of all the authors of the world translate truly
what those peasant seers know. Romantic? Yes.

But a challenge just the same. True wisdom starts
somewhere in the dirt and breaks across blue lakes
into clear skies. The other way around only leads
to pessimism and despair, or so it seems to me
who am limited after all, being merely the son of
Italian peasants and not having worked the soil
myself.

> I love you, Lord.
> But to say it, cheapens
> It somehow, and I
> Wonder if it is just my
> Own reluctance to
> Profess love too loudly
> And regularly in print,
> For outside of written
> Words I'm always saying,
> I love you. Funny thing
> About the written word: what
> We say always in every day
> Life when put down on
> The page doesn't work.
> Art is suggestion, is under-
> statement, is not saying
> What the reader should say
> You said even if you
> Didn't say it.

*C*an we ever give thanks enough for all the Lord has done for us? We begin to understand what thanks means the moment we stop comparing ourselves to others and look to what the Lord has done for us. He loves me in my uniqueness. He applauds when all other hands are still and when my own heart doubts my worth. And he suddenly becomes my audience, an audience of one, clamorous in his response.

Is this illusion? If it is, then saints do not exist and our own experience is illusion. For we all know men and women for whom God alone matters in the end. They live for him and they die for him, and everyone else they touch is freed by their selfless love and their own detachment from the obsession to succeed in human terms. They accept human praise and human love, but their world does not collapse when it is withdrawn. Behind everything is the good God and he stands in the wings and claps when there is silence from the gallery and boo's beyond the footlights.

And so we bow manfully whatever comes our way knowing who stands behind us, clapping for our effort and laughing when we take ourselves too seriously. And thanks rises to our lips as naturally as to a performer who has just brought down the house.

I think one of the reasons I write in this journal is because it keeps me from writing poetry which is always so inward-reaching and at times so close to madness. Here it is easier. You let the thoughts find themselves, and the emotions are sufficiently remote to make the act of writing safe. Most of the discipline of a journal is in making yourself write every day. The discipline of poetry is in the long periods of seeing and hearing and distilling in the mind and heart — then in trying to get it down on paper in tight, controlled images. No wonder I prefer these daily scratchings of the surface of the mind.

7. He Who Is There

The Lord is near. No words bring with them so much consolation and hope as these and so much despair when they seem not to be true. The Lord is near. That is precisely what everyone wants to believe and what so much of our experience seemingly belies. The Lord is so far from us sometimes because we don't recognize him or because we have already decided what those words mean. They mean that what I need more than anything else in life will be there. Usually that means love or intimacy of some kind. Rarely is it suffering or pain that we anticipate when we expect the Lord to be there.

And surely it cannot mean emptiness, loneliness, absence; for that is the very opposite of what we mean when we say that someone is near us or someone is there when we need him.

But the Lord is not just anyone, and his presence is often so much like absence that only one who has learned quiet and prayer would ever recognize him in the empty air that neighbors every man. Nor would that empty feeling in the heart ever lead the non-interior person to break through the emptiness to that fullness which is always surrounded by the protective shield of the void. The fullness of experience in God comes clothed in the disguise of absence, and only prayer can see beyond the disguise to the Lord whose nearness is as close as man's feeling of his absence. Absence and nearness in God are complementary terms in the sense that it is hard to distinguish one from the other. Furthermore, a feeling of nearness can mean that God has become my own emotional euphoria at the time.

In the end it is not my feelings that matter, but faith, faith that God is near no matter how I feel. As St. Paul says, there remain faith, hope, and love, and the greatest of these is love. Love flows from faith and hope and not from my feelings. Faith, hope, and love: a little trinity that makes me one and makes God near. This trinity alone makes it happen.

How do we pray without detachment, and how do we try to be detached without something to be detached from? We begin to pray well as soon as we realize that detachment is never an accomplished fact. It is never realized completely, nor perhaps should it be. In the process of trying to be reasonably detached, we pray. And prayer becomes more intense the more aware we are of our entanglements with things and people that distract us from God. This is not to say that things and people are not good. They are. But something has happened somewhere along the line; call it original sin or anything you like. The fact remains that most of our heartaches come from exaggerated attachments. And our peace flows from disinterested love, a love that does not attach itself and suffocate the beloved and the lover, as well.

It sounds old-fashioned to use words like "detachment," but our experience tells us daily that we are not really free and that there must be someone to love who transcends the *need* to be loved, a lover who invites rather than demands our love.

*F*or ten years now I have been returning to this slate grey tree that winters outside my window. Ten years! And I just realized that I don't even know for sure what kind of tree it is. I think it is a maple. But I do know the tree. Isn't it that way with so many of our experiences? We can't label them, and yet we know them as part of our daily experience.

Prayer is like that. People are always telling me that they would love to learn to pray. And then when I ask them how they pray now, they realize in telling me about it, that they have been praying for years. And I realize that they have been praying well. The reason they didn't think they were praying is that somewhere along the line they got it into their heads that prayer is some special, esoteric practice reserved for monks and mystics and has nothing to do with the lives of ordinary men and women. Nothing could be further from the truth. To pray is the privilege of every child of God. To speak to God is the gift won for every man by the death and resurrection of Jesus Christ himself. Jesus has made it possible for us to cry out, "Abba, Father."

Furthermore, the Gospels tell us over and over again that God hears, that he listens to what we say; and even more wonderful, that he answers. But that short statement, "he answers," is where many of us begin to doubt. "If God answers," we say, "why doesn't he answer *me,* now, when I need him, when I am begging for just one word from his lips?" When I am filled with these kinds of doubts, I realize that one of two things has happened inside me: Either I am not listening as I should, or I am listening only for what I want to hear from God.

The first problem is a difficult one to overcome because it means that I have to learn all over again how to be still and quiet inside, to rest in the Lord. And the second problem is even more difficult. If I am listening for only what I want to hear, then I have become selfish again, and I am listening only to myself. My prayer has turned into a monologue.

I write
And you leap onto the page, O Lord.
When I cannot write
Will you leap back into my heart?

8. Inner Sounds

I weary of taking pen in hand and trying to think on paper late at night. But always I remember that someone who is alone or afraid or just bored with life might someday read some small passage from these notes and take new courage or feel less alone or want to start living again. And that is why perhaps we pray when we are tired. Perhaps there is someone somewhere who needs our voice because his sticks in his throat, or he has given up praying altogether. And we cannot sleep until we pray in his stead. Each of us is capable of being an instrument for another's cry or another's song. We join with

Christ in redeeming our brothers and sisters. We
cannot redeem them, but we have it in our power
to effect some small change because we are joined
to Christ, their Redeemer and Lord. We do make
a difference for good or bad in all our fellowmen.

> In communion
>   With these woods again,
> These trees waiting always
>   At the edge of my property,
> The border of my solitude.

*L*ate at night when all
the sounds outside are quiet, the inner sounds
sometimes clamor to be heard, and we toss and
turn trying to still their demands. It is always the
same: They win for a while and finally sleep
comes — too late to bring that needed healing of
mind and body.

I reach out to you, O Lord,
And all I touch is my own emptiness,
Air and silence and the memory
That this kind of prayer never works for me.
When I am most in need,
Prayer never seems to help.

It only strengthens my own helplessness.
In your own way, in your own time
You will answer. That I know, that
I remember. So once again I lean on
Patience. I wait. Always there is
This waiting, this dread that I
Won't hold out. But I do, and
That is perhaps your answer.
We cannot stamp our feet or cry
And expect you to come running.
We only say, "Into your hands, O Lord."
And there is peace, for you are faithful
If not prompt, and you will answer
When you will answer. Amen. Alleluia.

God is love. That is all we know and all that matters in the end. For to say, "God is love," means that we are loved, and therefore we can love. Loving is all we can do that matters now or ever, and that is possible only because God is love. To love is to be, for God *is* love. When we love, we are, for God is because he loves. I don't understand any of this, but it consoles me.

I never seem to thank God as earnestly as I entreat him. Yet somehow I know that thanksgiving is really what prayer is about. God is so good and so faithful and that alone should make my whole life an act of thanksgiving. And when on top of that, I call to mind all that he has done in my life, the countless attentions, the growing within me, the obstacles he has removed, the gift of his presence, I blush at my ingratitude and indifference to him. Like the sparrows that have always been in my life, God is so present that I take him for granted. And therefore I thank God now for the Eucharist, that perfect act of thanksgiving in which his own Son gives thanks for me, even when at Mass my mind and heart are elsewhere. Without the Eucharist there is no thanksgiving; with it no further thanksgiving is necessary.

In the crises and sorrows of our lives one of the first questions we ask is, will someone be there, will anyone help to support us? In my own life this has become almost *the* definition of God: He who is there. Not just in crises, of course, but always. And yet it is most difficult to believe that he is there if there is not another human being there as well. Perhaps it is the weakness of my faith, but it is so hard to believe that God is here with me if there is no one else besides. When others stand with us and beside us, God shines forth in our midst. So maybe God keeps coming to us in the form of man.

One day is much like another in the spiritual life, in the search for God. But from time to time there is a sudden, unexpected revelation, or shining forth of God. You suddenly realize that God is everywhere, in everything and everyone. Call it insight, epiphany, baptism in the spirit, or any other name, it is the same experience: the God within me reveals his presence, fleetingly, and all the rest of my days are changed permanently. Something happens that I did not merit and that I cannot explain or communicate. But it is more real than any communicable experience, and I cannot formulate it or capture it in words. For to do so would be to have some hold on God, who cannot be captured in a phrase or formula. Nor can I, by remembering it, recapture the experience. It is gift; it is grace. The spirit blows where it will.

9. The Silence Inside

The silence of God. It is so deafening that if you are looking for a voice like any human voice that you can hear, you will surely give up on prayer and finally on God himself. God has spoken through the Scriptures and once for all through Jesus, his Son. And that is all in the past. Or is it? One of the surest effects of prayer is the conviction that God speaks to me here and now. His voice is not something I hear with my human ear, but something inside me that vibrates to the word of God spoken in utter silence at the core of my being. His voice is not a constant sound, but a presence that resonates somewhere deep within. And that felt presence, like the mere touch of someone we love, is sufficient to keep us going months on end.

In saying that this experience is a *felt* presence, I do not mean to imply that the experience of God is necessarily an emotional experience felt along the heart. It is more often than not a deep conviction that something has happened or is happening in my life that can be explained only by some divine epiphany, some shining forth, or revelation of the God who is always within me and who lets me experience that presence from time to time.

It is futile then to wait and listen for a voice from heaven to ring in the ear with some answer. The answer dwells within us, and now and then, it is uncovered and we know experientially that he is there.

"Credo ut experiar, I believe in order that I may experience." — St. Bernard.

*T*o most moderns "detachment" is a medieval, dehumanizing word that separates man from the goodness and beauty of creation. It means separation and alienation from the nitty gritty world. Nothing could be further from the truth. Like so much of the Christian mystery, detachment paradoxically means total involvement with life as we ordinarily understand that term. In order to be totally involved with you, I must somehow be detached from dependence on you; and if I am detached, you will not be enslaved by my involvement with you. It is as simple in essence and as difficult to achieve as that. And no one understands this perfect freedom and total involvement but he or she who has been loved by a saint. So once again the proof of words is verified in experience and without experience words are unconvincing, divisive, and problematical.

*G*od has called each of us to a special service of love and sharing. Most of the time that service is rendered in our ordinary, everyday living, but somehow we fail to see this fact and are constantly looking elsewhere to find ourselves. We think that our real call from God, our real identity is just around the next corner, that surely God has something other in mind for us than the commonplace demands of our own families and friends, of our own neighborhood, our own town. And because of this attitude we miss the real opportunities to discover who we really are, and we fail to grow to that stature in Christ that God intends for us. Jesus grew to manhood and holiness in the carpenter shop at Nazareth, learning to live with and to love his parents, relatives, and neighbors. We grow in love and holiness in the same way.

Lord, you draw me out.
You are more insistent
Than I want to believe
And so I fail to see my
Troubles as your probing,
Your way of saying that
I need to grow. I am
So blind to you that I
Actually pray for deliverance
From what you send
To make me whole.
Give me light to see by.

10. The People Outside

God cares. That is sufficient. It lasts. But always in the human condition there is more that we need: We need to know that God cares because other people care. In other words we are not isolated entities who relate exclusively to God. We are The Body of Christ, we are brothers and sisters in the Spirit; and that awareness of communion with others makes tangible our union with *the* other, God himself.

No other reality makes so powerful an impression on me as the fact that I am a member of the Body of Christ. That I am not alone, that I am

93

joined inextricably with all Christ's members, makes God's caring something more than words. In Christ's Body I find his spirit, and in his members I discover who he is. This alone keeps the spiritual life from becoming ethereal and egocentric. For that spirituality which narrows down to God and myself actually zeroes in on myself in the end, and God becomes what I make him out to be. The communion of saints saves the individual from union with himself, and God is revealed in incarnation, in enfleshment in all the members of his Body that I relate to, whether I realize it or not. The word was made flesh and dwelt, dwells, and will dwell among us.

The things and people we cling to imprison us; the things and people we love free us. The most liberating experience of all is to love something or someone and not at the same time want to possess the object of our love. True love allows the other its own freedom, yes, even desires that freedom; and in return the lover himself is free to love more and more selflessly.

Who, however, can achieve such love? Maybe no one can completely. But each one of us glimpses from time to time the exquisite joy of his own selflessness. If I am willing to love you and let you go whenever and wherever you wish, we are both free and our love grows. Otherwise, need and dependence replace love, and we grow tired of what all of this is costing us emotionally.

Some people learn this basic fact of life, and they become the saints we all know. Others never do learn it, and they are constantly caught in webs of their own making, unable to break loose and enjoy the freedom of the children of God.

What is the price of love? Is it not turning loose and letting go of what we think we cannot live without? That letting go, paradoxically, binds the beloved to us with hoops of steel, whereas the refusal to let go guarantees an early demise of love and the eventual loss of the beloved, and in the end, of ourselves. Somewhere in this simple truth of human relationships lies the mystery of the cross and of the resurrection. Or perhaps it is our own experience of love that makes the cross and resurrection of Christ believable.

*O*ne of the most frequent experiences of the person who prays is the feeling that God should be more present to him, more real, because of all the time and effort he has expended in trying to pray. But God, exquisitely coy lover that he is, never lets prayer become an end in itself or a vehicle by which we can capture him, or pin him down. There is no magic formula, no ritual that guarantees an instant God-experience. Every experience of God is a gift from God and he will not be tangibly present on demand.

What all this amounts to is that God is God and his will is his own. On the other hand he himself has told us through Jesus, his Son, that anything we pray for in Jesus' name will be given us, and that we should pray always and never lose heart. And so we continue to pray in faith and wonder why God doesn't come and satisfy our longing for him, the one gift we really need. The only solution that satisfies me is that God is a lover and as such intensifies our longing and love by his coyness. He draws near only to withdraw when we think we finally have him near us. And Faith replaces emotional experience with a new kind of experience, more real and more permanent than any transient feeling God might give us from time to time. Like real love faith endures when falling in love is over.

> When the wind returns
> The skies clear
> And my heart yearns
> To follow the wind.

*H*ow do I know my prayer is authentic and sincere? The age-old question. And today as always there is only one answer, and it is not in the prayer itself, but in what happens outside of prayer. Anyone can be "turned on" in prayer from time to time, especially in group prayer. But only the authentic person of prayer can be charitable. Again it is love that is the measure of anything in the spiritual life. If I love God, I will keep his two great commandments, and no one will be deceived about whether I do or not. Either I am charitable or I am not. I cannot fake it the way I can fake prayer or piety.

Therefore I should not worry about my prayer. That will only turn me inwards, make me selfish and self-preoccupied. But I *should* worry about

charity. Nothing takes me out of myself like trying to love my "enemy." Nor is anything more
impossible without God than true charity. The
measure of God's love for me might be the gifts
I receive in prayer, but certainly, the measure of
my love for him is how charitable I am to my
neighbor. God's love for me in prayer is authenti-
cated by my love for him in my neighbor.

11. Prayer and Play

Playfulness before God.
Each one of us has to be something of a fool,
something of a court jester before God if we are
not to take ourselves too seriously. And paradoxically, the more seriously we take God, the less
seriously do we take ourselves. If I center in on
God and make him the focus of my life, I gain
perspective on myself and can laugh at my own
seriousness, my own needless worries. God is

within me, but he is also apart from me and draws me out of myself. Therefore any prayer that drives me inward and makes me self-conscious is not really prayer but introspection.

This unhealthy introspection that sometimes passes for prayer is what makes many sensible people shy away from "prayer." People just can't take too much soul searching and navel gazing. Prayer is not self-analysis but self-liberation through concentration on and absorption in God. Most of us need to forget ourselves if we are ever going to find ourselves. Ironically, however, we moderns seem always to be trying to find ourselves and we end up like the dog trying to chase his own tail: we spin around in endless circles. And the whole business is taken very seriously.

What we need is some humor, some playfulness. In order to play, I have to forget myself; the game has to absorb my attention so fully that I forget how I am feeling or who is watching me or how well I am playing. And it is better to play a little every day than to play for protracted periods on the week-end. So with prayer; a little self-forget-fulness and meditation every day goes a long way. Praying and playing are somehow a part of the identical experience just as foolishness and wis-dom unite in the court jester. The pray-er and the jester don't self-consciously look over their shoul-ders to see who is watching.

Reaching out for God can be something like searching for your own identity: it is futile and self-defeating. In both cases it is better to reach out to other people and serve their needs. In so doing you will find God if you are seeking him and you will find yourself as well. Those who are forgetful of themselves are inevitably the ones we most admire and love. They are in possession of themselves and we know it. And yet we perversely seek for God where we are least ourselves, in our own self-centeredness.

Praise God for his ever-caring,
For his being there when we
Thought he was far away.
He is faithful and all time
Proves as much if we
Are patient enough to wait
For his past faithfulness
To register in our present
Consciousness. Awareness
Is the past catching up
With the present and
Disproving all our doubt.

2: Winter

12. Gray Days

The gray and wet of winter sometimes seeps into the soul and we pray for snow and ice to break the monotony of slate-colored days. Our life in God is like those gray days from time to time. Everything seems soggy and bogged down with water, and we feel heavy of heart. Wet days are for reaching out to others and not for meditating. Our inner weather is changed only by action, by charity, by breaking out of inward-looking melancholy. Yet so often we erroneously think that we must withdraw and think about our heavy mood and why it is upon us. Seldom, if ever, do we *think* ourselves out of depression. Rather we *act* ourselves out of it by taking other peoples' needs more seriously than we take our own. We don't change the weather outside by wishing it away; we ignore it and go about our work. Inner weather is handled much the same way.

There's something about snow on the landscape, something clean and protective, that insulates the heart and makes you feel secure. You don't notice the cold because usually you are inside a house or car looking out. And in a world of snow quiet subtly seeps into the heart.

The atmosphere for prayer is something like this experience. There must be silence outside, and the outside world must be somehow removed for the time of your watching. You then see your world from a new perspective. And even if it is cold and barren, you view it from the inner warmth of your own heart in union with God, and it looks white and beautiful again. Then you are ready to walk into the white snow made beautiful and warm by your new vision.

The joy of living in the Lord! When we first start living for God and with him, we are afraid that he isn't going to be enough, that we will eventually get bored with it all. And, of course, we would be bored if God were all we had to think about and talk to and live with all day. But God never demands that kind of total absorption from any of us. In fact our awareness of and love for him makes all our other loves possible and genuine.

I write this sentence only because I promised myself I'd try to write at least one sentence every day, and because one sentence leads to another. If only we could pray a little every day, even when it is only one word, for prayers like sentences lead into thoughts and eventually the heart hears and is lifted beyond the words to him who transcends all thought and every word.

*T*he world is wet with winter as Ash Wednesday draws near. The heaviness of water and the lightness of ashes mingle somehow in the soul seeking repentance. We are heavy with sins and attachments and long for that light touch of ashes that reminds us of the transitory nature of everyone and everything but God.

*T*his journal should not be a reflection *on* but a reflection from within, the sparrow within me talking, trying to sing.

*O*ne of the most terrifying experiences of life is the feeling that you have somehow been abandoned by God, that all your prayers have come to nothing, that perhaps there has been no one there all along and what you took for a relationship with God was in fact only yourself talking to yourself. Sooner or later this experience comes to everyone who tries to love God and to live a life of prayer. There is no way to prepare for it adequately or to avoid it, for it is God himself who calls you to this desert experience.

The only consolation when this barrenness is upon you is that it will pass, even though at the time the only thing you seem sure of is that it will not pass. And the only remedy is to turn vehemently (almost violently) to the service of others! The last thing in the world you feel inclined to do. What you want to do is withdraw into yourself and clamor at God's door begging for entrance. But if you leave that door and serve your brother and sister with all your heart, when you return, it will be standing open.

This service of others does not mean that you abandon prayer. Heaven forbid! It merely means that you try concentrating more on others than on yourself while continuing to pray in emptiness of spirit, not expecting any consolation or encouragement in return. And if you persevere in this routine (and it will seem terribly routine), the Lord will return to you and himself lead you back to his open door and welcome you inside. For he is faithful and he will not abandon you forever.

April afternoons in Assisi. It always seemed to be raining, and the shuttered afternoon siestas were dark with sleep and black clouds that settled permanently on Monte Subasio. For me this insulating effect was never one of melancholy. Rather I felt somehow protected and warm with my thoughts, despite the chill that seeped through thick rock walls into the little corner room where I wrote and prayed and stared out the French windows at the Rocca Maggiore with its somber background of rain-clouds. Perhaps I was so amazed and so thrilled to be in Assisi at all, that my inner weather counteracted and transformed anything negative that tried to invade it from without.

Many times since those idyllic three months in Assisi, I have traveled there again in memory, and what was past becomes present again, even embellished by imagination's coloring of those glorious days. I think this kind of experience speaks a great deal to us about what prayer is at times. Suddenly, without our expecting it, our inner weather is all sunshine and light, and all those outer things that previously affected our moods so drastically seem unable to touch our inner peace and well-being. But like a European jaunt or a long-awaited vacation, these periods never last for long. They are graces, gifts to be relished, to be gratefully enjoyed, even though we know those rainclouds will eventually sift into our souls and settle down for a while. And while they are there, we have memory's alchemy to keep us going.

13. Listening

The art of listening. How hard it is to cultivate. We seem to be able to listen to others only so long before we start talking ourselves, usually about ourselves. It is that way with prayer, too. The hardest part is the listening, the quiet, the patience it takes to be still and wait upon the Lord. We always want to start talking, and yet what more can we say beyond the words Christ gave us in the "Our Father"? If we spent our time in prayer saying the "Our Father" once and then listening for the remainder of the time we set aside for prayer, it would be one of the best disciplines possible in learning to pray.

But we are uncomfortable with silence, with waiting for the other to speak. This is strange, really, because we all know how much more is communicated in silent communion with someone we love than in a plethora of words that soon seem empty and repetitious. God, like all lovers, speaks louder in the quiet of his presence than in words spoken in a rush of emotion. And he hears us better in our silent awareness of and concentration on him than in a multiplicity of words.

There are times, of course, when we must pray in a rush of words and emotion, in times of great trouble or joy, for instance. But that is more for our sake than his. He knows what we are going to say before we say it. The saying it, however, helps us and heals us in the release of pent up sorrow or lifts us up in the release of too much joy or gratitude. Generally, however, lovers speak in silence and hear in silence, and words only complicate the purity of their communion.

Prayer is not only a need that each of us has; it is also a power. Jesus has told us that whatever we ask in his name, his Father will give us. And because prayer is a power, it is also a responsibility and a challenge. It is a responsibility because through prayer we can join with Christ in redeeming the world. If we pray only for ourselves or about ourselves, we have not yet learned to pray, for prayer is outward-reaching and all-embracing. A good barometer of where we are in the spiritual life is whether or not our prayer reaches out to all people. If my prayer centers in mainly on myself, then that is where I am. The true pray-er accepts Christ's challenge to join with him in opening his arms to all men. And as his prayer becomes more cosmic and other-centered, so does the thinking and attitude of him who prays.

I once heard Gabriel Marcel say, "I found God in another person in whom God dwelt." I remember how stunned I was to hear this complex, deep man say something so simple. I had expected some profound answer about his search for God through the circuitous route of his own existential thought. Instead, a simple statement and this in answer to a question from the audience after a penetrating lecture on the theater of the absurd. A young man rose in the audience and asked Professor Marcel how he had found God, and in contrast to the profundity of his lecture, he said that he had found God in another person; it was as simple as that. This answer was something anyone could understand.

Each one of us, whether he realizes it or not, is a living symbol of the presence of God in the world. By who we are and how we act we can either build up or tear down the Kingdom of God. God has chosen to act through men, first through his son, Jesus, and then through all the members of his Mystical Body. That God is alive and well is most evident in those who live through him and with him and in him. No greater compliment could be given a man than that someone should say he found God in him.

When we finally come to love ourselves, something happens inside us that makes humility possible. I cannot humble myself if I think myself worthless or unworthy of love. It is only he who recognizes his own worth and his own lovableness who can even *think* of humbling himself. If we try to humble ourselves before we love ourselves, we only sink more deeply into depression and a low self-esteem. What most of us need is to know we are loved, to know we are worthwhile. And that is precisely what only Jesus can do for us through the Spirit that he sends us.

We pray and worry, worry and pray over some heavy burden of mind or body, and nothing happens. Time passes. And all our hope rides away with time. Then, just when the last car of time is passing away, with all our hope inside, the burden is lifted just in time for us to run lightly again and catch the last car. Why God lets us wait for that final car is a mystery, but perhaps that is what faith and hope are about — waiting. No instant answers, no instant changes. No ride on the first seat of the first car in a train, but just making the last car of a moving train with one seat left. Waiting and watching all those cars go by, too heavy to jump aboard, makes every ride a miracle and every leap something only God can accomplish in us. And we realize our dependence on him and his faithfulness to us.

You, O Lord, are the one
Who calls my name
I hear you in the place
Called prayer, where
Names are necessary
Only in the beginning.

Prayer lets you experience the gospel paradox of losing yourself in order to find yourself. The more you lose yourself in contemplation of God, the more yourself do you really become. You come away from prayer more convinced that you are someone special, having just talked with God. You know your name, and it sounds good to the ear. How this happens is a mystery, but it has its counterpart in human love. When I lose myself in someone I love, I feel more free, more independent than when I am alone; and I am full, not empty, when I give myself away.

*S*implicity of style. In art as in life simplicity has its own charm. The simple word is often the exact word that triggers complex responses within us. The simple man, we feel, has somehow passed through complexity and confusion, and his simplicity is really transcendence and victory over the inessential entrapments of life.

In prayer we learn the simple word that effects and flows from a simple life. Our life and prayer are so intertwined that they, too, become a new simplicity of word and act. There is a Chinese proverb on the wall of the children's museum in Boston that sums up simply what I am trying to say so falteringly:

"I hear . . . and I forget.

I see . . . and I remember.

I do . . . and I understand."

Very simply, that is prayer and action integrated.

We strain hard at times, listening for that one word, that voice of assurance from the other side. And when the strain becomes too much for us, we go back to feverish activity and diversion convinced that prayer is not for us, that it is a gift God gives to special souls. Then something draws us back again, some hope that this time it will work. What draws us back is something inside us, something that was there from the beginning. And that movement from within, that drive is really the voice of God that we were listening for "out there" somewhere. In other words, more often than not, the voice of God is a force within us propelling us toward God. It is God himself leading us to himself.

But we remain frustrated because we are never satisfied with what happens at that rendezvous called prayer. If there *is* satisfaction of any kind, it is so short-lived that we wonder if it was worth it. And yet we return to prayer again and again. And in the returning we notice something happening, not during prayer exactly, and not all of a sudden. But gradually something has been happening to us. *We* are changing. A peace and calm is settling into our lives and we begin to hear God's word in Scripture in a way we didn't before. It is somehow more personal, more directly related to our lives. The Mass takes on a new meaning, and we yearn for frequent union with Christ in the Eucharist.

In brief, what we had been expecting to happen suddenly in prayer, had been happening gradually in our daily lives.

14. Open Spaces

Sometimes the reason we cannot pray is that we haven't any space left in our lives. We are psychologically, spiritually, and perhaps even physically hemmed in. We are moving at such a frenetic pace and the press of responsibilities and the people who make inroads on our time and energy is so great that we really haven't any space left for ourselves. If we try then to use the little time we have left for prayer, we come to prayer already exhausted and tense.

It would be better, if such is our situation, to take some positive steps to reduce the pressures in our lives and provide some extra space for relaxation. And certainly before trying to pray at the end of the day it is better to unwind first from the pressures and tensions of work. In providing space and relaxation we are making remote preparations for the calm and tranquility necessary for listening to God.

Prayer and life are so intimately intertwined that we must be sensible in both areas if we are to achieve the kind of integration that God intends for us. Most of us tend to so over/extend ourselves in work and attending to the needs of others, that we leave little to God. We should put our lives and the worry about them more and more into God's hands and spend more time in prayer with him. The result will be an increased alertness and ability to do our daily tasks with energy and enthusiasm and a growing awareness of God's care and providence in our daily lives.

*D*oes anything happen in prayer that is not just the result of relaxation and a kind of self-hypnosis? Is there in fact a real contact with God? And if there is, how do we know it? These are questions I have never been able to answer to my own satisfaction, and yet I know that something does happen in prayer. At least I know that God hears, that he answers my prayers. But that I have ever heard him, I don't know. I do know that from time to time his word in Scripture is sweet to my heart and I feel that he is reaching into the very center of me. And at the beginning of my journey to him I felt his presence everywhere. But how much of that sweetness and consolation was God and how much was my own enthusiasm is hard to say.

Ultimately what I *can* say is that I know God most when he withdraws, when I no longer feel anything. It is something he does, suddenly, without warning, and then I know that he was certainly there because of the emptiness and panic of his leaving. And I understand that his presence is not heard or seen except in its removal. Then I know that loneliness which makes for hell.

In saying God is known only in his leaving, I am making an extreme statement which must be qualified. There are from time to time, but very rarely, deep and very real experiences of God. These experiences are untranslatable, but they are attested to by many spiritual writers and mystics. Usually, these experiences come early, if not at the very beginning, of one's conversion to the interior life and the memory of them sustains us for years. But they are by no means the staple of the spiritual life. Our life in God is nourished primarily by word and sacrament and not by felt religious experience. This is why I make the seemingly extravagant statement that God is known experientially only in his leaving. And I am speaking, of course, of ordinary men and women and not of special people like Moses whom "the Lord knew face to face" (Dt. 34: 10).

*L*ate at night when I struggle to pen a few words on prayer, I realize how little I know about prayer. And that is perhaps why I continue to try and write about it. I feel that if I try writing about it often enough, it may come clear to me. I am probably deluding myself and should be spending these late evening hours praying instead of writing about prayer. Or do I pray with pen in hand? Maybe that is the trouble; I'm writing letters to God instead of talking to him. But that seems how I best communicate with him at times, because writing leads into real prayer, just as writing to a loved one brings him or her to mind, and the person becomes present as we write and see in the mind's eye the one we're writing to. Writing for me is remote preparation for prayer. Each person finds his own avenue to God in that which prepares his heart to listen and speak to the Lord.

For a few years now I have used a little memory device to help people who are learning to pray. The memory help is the word SPORT, each letter of which stands for a different step in prayer.

The "S" stands for silence, probably one of the most difficult parts of prayer. In order to pray well, we must become interiorly silent; we must let all our tensions and preoccupations drain away and let a calm and soothing spirit descend upon us. Just trying to achieve this quiet of mind and heart might take up most of our prayer time, but it is necessary to all that follows.

The "P" stands for purification. If I am going to pray well, I must be able to purify my heart, and that means I must be able to forgive. I must try, at least, to forgive all the hurts I have received in my life. I must even try to forgive myself as God forgives me. If I cannot forgive someone, then my prayer remains on that level, and it does not deepen and grow until I can forgive.

The "O" stands for openness. Once I am interiorly still and have forgiven my neighbor from my heart, then I am ready to be open to God's word. I can open the Scriptures and read what the Lord is saying to me, or I can just remain silent and let him speak in the depths of my heart.

The "R" stands for response. What does God want me to do? What is he saying to me now and how am I going to respond to his word? All prayer leads somehow into concrete action, for prayer and life are one act of love.

The "T" stands for talking. Only now am I ready to talk to God. Notice that up till this time I have been quiet; I have been listening, open to God. The "T" could also stand for Thanksgiving, letting thanks rise to my lips for all the Lord has done for me, especially in this brief period of prayer that he has granted me.

This is one simple way of praying, probably not the best, and certainly not the only way, but it may be a beginning for some.

*T*here is an old saying that God can write straight with crooked lines. How often each of us has experienced something like that in his or her life!

I write, not because I
know, but because I do not know. In like manner
I pray, not because I know how to pray, but because I don't. This is not false humility but the
truth. Those who wait until they know, will never
write, and those who sit back and wait for the
gift of prayer, for some grand inspiration, will
pray very little. The pray-er is a searcher; he
reaches out for the God he loves, most of the
time clumsily and without much satisfaction.

And through all of this he is praying in the
Spirit. The reason I make this last statement is
that some falsely believe they are praying in the
Spirit only when they are filled with joy and
enthusiasm and when they tangibly experience
the influx of the Spirit and break into sponta-
neous praise and thanksgiving. Nothing could be
further from the truth. Life is not a continuous
celebration. It is rather a rhythm of joys and sorrows, certitude and doubt, fullness and emptiness,
intimacy and loneliness, turning inward and turning outward. And our prayer reflects this same
rhythm as did the prayer of Jesus.

Whenever I pray, no matter how I am feeling,
the Spirit prays with me and within me with
"unutterable groanings."

15. Running

Every once in awhile a person who is trying to pray is tempted to leave everything and go away into some wilderness to be alone with God. He thinks, yes, there I could really pray; there my prayer would soar to heaven on wings. We would all like to withdraw from life awhile, and from time to time it is good to retreat with God; but our prayer is best and most sincere when we pray where we are.

Prayer that rises spontaneously from our every-day lives is our real prayer, the real gauge of how earnestly we are trying to live in God and for him. What I do and how I act from day to day is more indicative of who I am than the extraordinary things I do, and how I pray from day to day says more about my interior life than infrequent spurts of devotion or a period here and there of intense prayer and meditation.

*S*omeone, a lovely lady and poet, sent me a collection of Italian poems. This one I love. It is called, "E tu Iddio," "You, God." The poet, Danilo Dolce; the poem written in 1924, the translation:

YOU, GOD

You, God
Because of whom I walk in this boundless sky
among clouds of worlds
You are lonelier, poorer than I;
I have seen you wince under the surgeon's scalpel
removing an ulcer from your bowels.
I have seen You dead drunk
staggering empty-eyed,
I have seen You
tense pushing a laden wheel-barrow,
jump for joy over new pockets
over shiny shoes
and call out to me, and stretch out Your hands
happy over a smile and a little kiss.

Those sparrow-like eyes of yours
make me sad.
In order to live, I must be a brother
and a father to You.
And wipe your running nose
and support you in your faltering steps,
build you a stout house
of solid stone in fine plumb, and heal you
if your head limply resting on my knees
burns with fever,
and fetch you bread, soup
and honey and the fruit you like:
it is my way of adoring you.

*L*ately I find myself
thinking more about prayer and praying less. A
lot of people I know are like that; instead of doing, they think. Pray-ers do this frequently because in thinking, they can remain locked up in
themselves; but to actually pray, they have to
break out and lift their minds and hearts to God.
They have to try and communicate and listen to
the other, and that is difficult. The person who

thinks about prayer is like the person who talks about writing, but doesn't write. He does not know writing at all because he hasn't experienced it in process but only as a finished product to be analyzed. The real pray-er often doesn't know how to talk about his prayer and doesn't really think about it that much; he prays, and that is sufficient.

If you don't pray, God is a name; if you do, he is a person.

Lord, I used to think
That you hid from me.
But lately I realize
More and more that
I'm the one to blame:
I don't play games well.
I keep missing you,
Keep being blind and
Bad at finding people
And things and you.

I keep writing
After midnight,
Hoping I might
Help you, biting
Your fingernails,
Sleepless, afraid.

16. Letting God Be Himself

In God's hands. How often we say that and want to be able to believe it. One of the most difficult aspects of prayer is that it demands so much faith and trust in God. We would much prefer doing everything ourselves rather than putting things in God's hands. It seems hard enough just to stop working and worrying long enough to spend time with God in prayer, let alone having the trust to turn over our lives to him and letting him "worry" for us.

Our life with God is an intimate relationship with a person, and it works much the same as the relationships we have with others. If we have to do everything ourselves and never trust anyone else, we find ourselves not only doing everything alone but after awhile we *are* very much alone. We have no friends, and it's hard to talk to people or listen to them. If, however, we work with others and let them share with us, we grow in an awareness of our essential communion with other people; and because we have shared responsibilities and play, sorrow and joy, we find it much easier to communicate verbally and non-verbally as well.

From this very human fact of our experience we should learn something about our relationship with the most important person of our lives. We have to let him share by trusting him and letting him into the practical, day-to-day side of our lives. We have to let him act. And if we do, then our prayer takes on all kinds of new dimensions. We have much to talk to God about because he has been sharing the whole day with us. He has been there, so there are a lot of things we feel we don't have to say. We can be silent together in the day's failures and/or successes.

In order to reach this stage of prayer, however, we have to be able to put at least some things in God's hands and trust him. How easy to say; how hard to do.

The man who can put things in God's hands and trust him grows daily in the knowledge that for him who loves God, all things work together unto good. Out of the great sorrows and pain of my life come goodness and beauty and insight I never had before. Someone, I think it was Leon Bloy, once said that there are places in the human heart which do not yet exist, and into the heart comes suffering, that they may have existence. Out of such a heart prayer rises naturally as thanksgiving for the wholeness of everything that is, as a hymn to God who draws good even out of what we thought was evil.

No matter how much I pray, I still end up saying, most of the time, "Lord, teach me to pray." I suppose in one sense we never learn to pray, we never feel that we have arrived. If we did feel that way, we would stop praying, for we would possess what prayer yearns for, an experienced union with God. Our yearning and never really learning help us to keep praying.

*T*hose who carry the sick to the pool of Bethesda. That is the image that crosses my mind when I think of those saintly men and women whose daily prayers are mostly for others. They lift people up and carry them to the healing pool of Bethesda, to the living waters of Christ himself. There are so many who do not pray or do not know how to pray, and they lie helpless right next to the water that could give them new life. And we, by our prayers for them, bring them to that water.

*W*hy do we pray when no answer seems forthcoming? Is it because we hope against all odds that we will hear the answer we are expecting? Or is it because we have "heard" something before and hope against hope that we will hear it again? Both responses sound cynical, but both are true sometimes when we bite our lips and pretend that we are hearing God and talking to him the way other people say they do.

Most of our anxieties about prayer come from what preachers, authors, and our acquaintances say they experience. It is usually so different from the darkness that we walk in, from the emptiness we feel most of the time. Like so many other things in our lives, we should trust our own experience, as poor and simple as it may seem at times. God comes to each one of us in his own way and time and in the manner best suited to each person. He doesn't come according to some manual or primer of prayer, but according to our need and readiness for him.

And so we keep praying, remembering how he came before and trying to ignore the self-proclaimed "pray-ers" who tell us there is something wrong with us, that we are putting some barrier in the Lord's way. We keep praying because common sense tells us God is more loving and more aware of who we are and what we need than those advisers in the spiritual life who are more like Job's accusers than wise men of the spirit.

God loves us. If only we could hold to that above everything else. We long to believe it. We want above all else to profess it. We know it is true. But others sometimes make us doubt it because they seem not to care. And, of course, what we can see and hear and touch moves us more than what we believe. It is only when belief conquers experience that we are truly men and women of faith.

T he search for God ends up in the end being God's search for you. You take so many wrong turns just where you might have met him at some corner of your life. But in the end he surprises you by finding you looking for him in the wrong direction. God comes your way, no matter how far afield you are. That is the story of God; he goes out of his way. You are that important; that is the story of man.

G od does not give us grace for the future, but for the present. I become more and more convinced of this: If I pray for something that is in the future, my worries seem only to increase. But if I pray and live each day as it comes, God gives me the grace to bear the burden of each particular day. I wonder if other people experience the same thing?

17. A Bow in His Hands

There is a point of surrender in our lives that we yearn for and strive for but seldom reach. And that is to turn completely to God and let ourselves go, to be able to put everything in his loving hands. This is the final stage of our relationship with God, a relationship which Nikos Kazantzakis put so succinctly in his autobiography, *Report to Greco*. The book begins with these words: "Three kinds of souls, three prayers:

1) I am a bow in your hands, Lord. Draw me, lest I rot.

2) Do not overdraw me, Lord, I shall break.

3) Overdraw me, Lord, and who cares if I break!"

I do not think these are three kinds of souls necessarily; they are stages in our journey to God. We begin enthusiastically, then we become afraid, then we surrender; and in that surrender we return to our first enthusiasm again.

Most of the time I find it difficult to pray simply because I am too concerned with my own affairs. I insist on setting everything right all by myself. And I see the same fault in so many others. We form a large part of mankind, I am afraid. If we "have to" do everything ourselves, we do not realize our fundamental dependence on God, and most of our activity is fruitless toil that exhausts us rather than fulfills us. God's will becomes secondary to our own.

We must, of course, work, but the attitude we bring to work makes all the difference. As St. Francis admonished his friars, we must work so as not to extinguish the spirit of prayer and holy devotion to which all things must be subservient.

People were always expecting Jesus to be someone other than he was. They thrust their own image of the Messiah upon him and insisted that he be a king like other kings they knew. How much pain and frustration that must have caused him, knowing that he couldn't be what they wanted him to be. And the more he tried to be who he really was, the more they rejected him and misunderstood him.

We, too, experience this kind of suffering, because we seldom measure up to what others expect us to be. And, as always, we know that Jesus has been there before us. And that makes it somehow important that we keep trying to be ourselves.

3: Spring

18. Springtime of the Soul

On clear days in early March, when the wind blows all day long, everything seems cleaner somehow, and it is easy to puff up your lungs and inhale spring. There are soul days like that, too. Something clicks inside and everything seems bright and clear again. Then joy and gratitude rise to the lips spontaneously, and it is easy to praise God for all the lightness you feel within. It is spring in your soul.

March Snow

An indignant robin
Ruffles his feathers
And broods darkly
Over Ohio weather
That surprised him
With snow on his
Comfortable perch.
Sparrows aren't so
Indignant to snow.

March Wind

The wind is back.
Suddenly without warning
It blows through the mind.
Will it clear the clouds
Or only chill the air and
Bring a fresh pall of snow?

Winter Woods

Winter woods, when
Did you become so silent?

God is as close to us as we are to ourselves. We reach out to him and go on pilgrimage to him and search for him in other people, and all along he is more close to us than anything or anyone or any place where we are trying to find him.

The reason we can't find God in ourselves is that we are out of touch with our true selves. We are uncomfortable with who we are; and until we learn to love ourselves, the search for God wearies us and we are constantly being frustrated. The paradox in all of this is that we cannot set out deliberately to love ourselves in order to find God. We have to somehow lose ourselves by giving up the search for God and for ourselves. That in itself sounds like insanity to anyone who hasn't experienced the futility of trying to find himself and God any other way.

The other paradox is that we lose ourselves through others, but we need solitude to do that. We need to have human relationships, but we also need breathing space from others. There is a balance here somewhere which only the Spirit of God reveals to us once we let go a little and learn to hold ourselves and others more gently. If you hold on too tightly, you and others and God all slip through your fingers and become remote. God is as close to you as you are to yourself and others. Hold yourself gently and the rest will follow.

Beach

Bodies huddled together
On the beach
So far from one another's
Reach.

How often in prayer we
keep coming back to ourselves,
our own worries and concerns,
and forgetting altogether him
we are talking to and listening
for.

19. Being and Doing

S ometimes we fritter our lives away waiting for something to happen from our prayer. We fret and worry and pray desperately when what we need to do is to make some decision, to make some move forward from our entrenched predicament. We need perhaps to reach out to someone other than God for help, guidance, or support. Prayer must initiate or continue some action in our lives or it degenerates into a security blanket of some kind, that seems to justify our doing nothing but praying.

In other words, we are back to the old truism that prayer and action go together and you can't have one without the other.

Decision

Now, Lord, it is time.
I will away from me
Into you and your world.
As much as I fear you,
It is too much for me
Here alone with myself.

Lord,
I don't have to pray to you
Somewhere out there beyond
These scattered rain clouds
That threaten the beach with dark.
I'm talking to you right now,
Right here inside me. Clouds
Don't matter really, or anything
Else that is out there beyond me.

Writing again.
That is important,
More important
Than sun and sea
And warm beaches:
They *are*; writing *does*.

*T*he journey into myself
is the most frightening of all adventures.

*C*an anyone make
us conscious of God but God himself? Conscious
in the sense of aware, perhaps, but consciousness
that implies an experience of the living God, only
God can effect in us.

> Fly the wind
> Before the calm;
> There will be time
> For a healing balm
> After the climb.

Walking the beach in the early sun
We suddenly lift our heads and run
Moved by some crazy impulse to speed.
What we really need, who knows?
It's what we do remembering the blows
We've suffered and still we aren't freed.

*T*he secret is in letting go and trusting God. Only that kind of surrender makes any sense for the Christian. Otherwise he really isn't a follower of Jesus, whose whole life was a handing himself over to the Father. Not my will but thine be done. . . . Into thy hands I commend my spirit. . . . I come to do the will of him who sent me.

We fight that kind of surrender and resist it. Then one day we wake up and realize that letting go is the only answer. And waking up is pretty much what happens. Everything before that insight was a sleeping away of our lives in fear and trepidation. Then we jump out of bed and start living fully for the first time. Nothing matters from then on but God's will, and God himself absorbs our failures and our successes, and we praise him no matter what happens.

*T*he kingdom of heaven is within you. Why then should you falter? Trust him who reigns inside you. Surrender yourself to him and believe that he cares almost as much as you do about your life!

Whenever I write sarcastically about how little we trust God, it helps me to see again how little *I* trust him. It is *I* who think I care more about me than he does, that I have to do everything so that someone in heaven will notice, maybe. And in truth he is here all along loving me and sharing everything with me. And not he alone but the whole kingdom of heaven is with me and for me. Why then should I ever lose heart? Turn inward in prayer—there is God and his kingdom.

I stand in the woods
And weep for the wind
That blew through my mind
When woods were somewhere
To go that mattered.
Now I walk through them
For exercise.

Where have all the words flown
That came so easily to mind
So short a time ago? I search
The skies for their winging back:
Nothing there but blue and grey.

20. Prayer and Madness

"A man needs a little madness or else he never dares cut the rope and be free"—Zorba.

Lord, I pray for this
Freeing madness, this
Unbinding bond with you.
But I hold myself too tightly
For this ever to happen
Unless you take my arms
From clutching myself
And let them embrace others
Instead. I yearn for this
But keep my arms around
me tighter than ever.

Frimom the play, *Zalmen,
or The Madness of God,* by Elie Wiesel.
"Inspector: And you Rabbi? Which side are you
on? The question or the answers?
Rabbi: I am on the side of prayer.
Inspector: What is prayer; question or answer?
Rabbi: Both. Question for whoever believes he
has found an answer. Answer for whoever
struggles with the question."

If we were to attain
what we reach for in prayer, then prayer would
be unnecessary. We reach out to God in prayer,
and usually we are frustrated. Some books on
prayer make me wonder if the author isn't exag-

gerating his own experience or putting into the book what he would like his prayer-life to be rather than what it really is. An active prayer-life does not mean an on-going experience of God. On the contrary, it usually means an on-going hunger for the God who seems not to be there. Like everything else worthwhile in the human condition, prayer is difficult and seldom brings with it the comfort and fulfillment so many authors say it is supposed to bring.

And still we continue to pray, just as we continue to love even though love is not everything it is romanticized to be. The need to pray like the need to love comes from deep within and I suspect more people pray than anyone would dare believe. Not everyone has faith, of course, but with or without faith, people pray or want to pray.

Anyone who embarks on the journey of prayer should know at the beginning that he is in for all the disillusionment and frustration that a long journey involves. He may not even persevere to the end; but even

if he does, the way will not be easy. It will, however, be a challenge to and an adventure of the spirit. What this means in practical terms is that it takes a certain inner toughness to enter into prayer and persevere in it.

God hears me. How hard that is to believe at times. We want to believe it with all our heart, and so we pray mightily and storm heaven with our cries. And the silence terrifies us. We turn inward to the God who dwells within and there is only emptiness there. And yet we believe. We know he is there because the mustard-seed faith we do have is stronger than the mountain of doubt that threatens it. That is the only way I can explain how my little faith continues to win over the emptiness and doubt that seems so large, so terrifying. God hears me pray and beg for a strong, courageous faith, and he keeps sending mustard seeds, and they are sufficient. I suppose we always want more than we really need while God continues giving us our daily bread.

21. Song of the Sparrow

The sparrows are all gone.
Or so I thought. Actually
I forgot to look for them.
They're always there
Beyond the imprisoned self.
God is that way, too.
Only he's inside the self
As well as out there.
So close yet so far
From the self turned in
Upon itself.

I pray you, Lord,
Not to let me forget

The sparrows, for they
Remind me that I
Am more to you
Than many sparrows
Who mean so much to me.

Behind everything
And within everything
Are you, O Lord.
And we do not
See and hear you
Except in those things
And persons you
Inhabit. Why then
Do we expect a word
From you directly?
Things and people
Should be sufficient,
But sadly they are not.

Dear Lord,
I want you
And only you;
But somehow
You want me
To have you
Only through
Others. Who
Am I to want
What you do not

Want for me?
This mystery
I will never
Understand:
That you want
To be known
Through man
And when we
Try to find you
Apart from others,
You are not there
For finding.

Spring Rain

Dark rain flooding
New green fields and trees,
Washing past the leaves
Into dark roots.
I watch the rain
And feel it washing me,
Running down my body
Into soil without roots
Of mine. My roots are
Inside where rain
Never enters. I pray
For inner rain, O Lord,
Don't send me
Sterile thunder.

*T*he mystic cannot live without divine nearness. Its absence drives him to madness or to a human love which he sees as a betrayal, innocent though it may be.

*G*od's love, when it comes to us through other people, overwhelms us so. The reason is, I think, that God is always more convincing enfleshed, and that is what Incarnation is all about. The Incarnation was not a once-upon-a-time event. It re-occurs each time we find God in another human being. People like you and me *are* in fact the Body of Christ.

22. Darkness and Light

Sometimes prayer is nothing more than the search for the proverbial "light at the end of the tunnel." We walk in darkness, groping and stumbling and not really believing there is a light or an end to the tunnel. At times like these we can do no more than continue stumbling and groping. In other words, we continue to pray, despite the darkness and the seeming hopelessness of it all. Only in this way do we reach the new light that God is holding out to us.

If we stop and give up, we remain in darkness until God himself drills through the earth and lights our way where we are. This light, however, is not the light that would have been ours had we continued walking the tunnel he himself prepared for us. And God becomes the great miracle-worker who rescues me, not the lover who waits patiently

at the end of the tunnel for my own love and
devotion to bring me to him. The relationship is
different because I have not let love have its way.
Only in perseverance through darkness does love
grow.

Lord, let me find you
When I am alone
And when I'm with others.
Do not let my solitude
Turn into loneliness,
Or my communion
With others become
Separation from you.
Alone or peopled
My heart puts you
In the center.

The heart reaches out
For God, first *around others*
And then *through* them
To him who dwells inside
The people we love.
It is a journey frought
With indirections
And the temptation
To stop with the other
Who is not God,
But who can lead us to God
If we love enough.

Jesus returns to us through his Holy Spirit. He is born in us and we manifest him to others as Mary did when she surrendered herself to the Holy Spirit and said, "Behold the handmaid of the Lord; be it done unto me according to thy word."

Mary is *the* human model of love: Because of her special relationship to the Holy Spirit, she, like Don Quixote in the song *The Impossible Dream*, had to love others pure and chaste from afar, and this included her love for Joseph, her husband. This does not mean that she never touched St. Joseph or held him, but that their love never achieved the union that all married love seeks. The reason for this is not that there is something wrong with sex, but because she was already married to the Holy Spirit.

The Holy Spirit overshadowed Mary and she became the mother of Jesus, the mother of God himself. Mary then becomes the model of all virginal love, of all celibate love. Because the virgin is wed to God himself, his or her love for others never achieves union. But again this does not mean that the virgin stops loving or keeps others at a "safe" distance. In fact because of the virginal person's deep love of God he or she can love others more deeply and more really than can those who have excluded God from their lives.

For the person wholly dedicated to God, love becomes the center of life. The virgin's love is the love of Christ himself loving his brothers and sisters in a warm yet non-possessive way.

23. A Clearing in the Woods

here is an image from early America that flashes across my mind whenever I think of contemplation or meditation. It is an image of a pioneer hacking down trees, trying to make for himself a small clearing in the wilderness, a clearing for living and planting, a place where things will grow. That is what a pray-er must do. He must make out of the maze of his daily living a small clearing where he can be at peace, where God can plant the seed of his word, where man can watch things grow. It is a task as difficult as subduing the wilderness and it is never finished because the wilderness constantly creeps in again with weeds and undergrowth that threaten to choke out what was cultivated with so much care. But this clearing in the woods is necessary if one is ever to learn the art of prayer.

How this clearing is achieved is as individual as man himself. And the woods themselves have a fascination that often prevents us from even wanting a clearing. As the poet Robert Frost says, "The woods are lovely, dark and deep."

We lose our gift for tinkering (and it is a gift) the more seriously we take ourselves and the world we live in. And ironically it is the tinkerer inside each of us that, once freed, makes it possible for us to be serious without becoming self-conscious and self-preoccupied.

The tinkerer in us says, "Work with your hands," "Go to bed early, so you can get outside and romp before breakfast." The tinkerer inside is the little boy or girl we thought we left behind. The tinkerer is that melancholy twinge we get as we drive by the little farm we'd like to have. It's feeling the soil beneath our feet again and seeing dirt under our fingernails and knowing that sanity is somewhere there in the dark soil and in our working near it.

The tinkerer is ourselves at play, at contemplation, at work we like to do. If we could but free the tinkerer in us, he would kill the demons of the mind that plague us with a seriousness gone mad.

Writing is a form of prayer. I never seem to learn to pray, Lord, so I take pen in hand and hope these few lines will help hold you. You are always near, but I somehow drift away, caught up in my own preoccupied self. I'm always preparing to meet something you would take care of for me if only I let you, if only I would trust you. I am your own poor instrument. Take me up in your presence and show me what to do, for I am so ignorant of what I should do, of what you want me to do; I look everywhere for signs of your will that fit my own. They never substitute for your own voice deep inside my heart.

Reaching out to God sometimes involves first reaching out to others. There are two great commandments: The love of God and the love of neighbor. And at times the reason our love of God seems sterile is that we have forgotten how to love our neighbor. The other side works, too, of course. When the love of neighbor begins to wane, we have somehow forgotten how to love God. But it is the love of God which most often seems dead in our lives. So we must reach out to others if we hope to rekindle the love of God. These two commandments and these two dimensions of our lives work together and there is never one love without the other.

Night Thoughts

The way the wind sounded
In the trees last night
Reminded me somehow
Of other nights that now
In memory are full of light.
Strange how life is rounded
By darkness becoming light.

*C*ontemplative prayer is possible only where there is quiet and where there is time that is unhurried. Quiet and time. Both are more internal than external. I must be quiet on the inside and the time I take out for prayer must be time for "wasting," time just for me. This attitude of mind is not easy to acquire, for always there is something more important to do, or there is something gnawing away at my attention, and try as I may, I just can't become quiet inside. And yet if I continue trying to attain this kind of tranquility, it happens from time to time like a sweet gift from heaven, that I *am* caught up in the silence and timelessness of God.

Prayer

"I love you"
Is too direct
But it is all.
You need me
To say it,
So I do.
On paper
It looks and
Sounds as cheap
As not saying it
Really is.

*T*his journal is coming to an end and I cannot understand why. It is dying of itself, so I suppose there is no more to say, or at least that I have nothing more to say. It is unsatisfying somehow, and yet it is complete because there is no more. You can only listen to a sparrow so long, and perhaps this is already much more of sparrow-talk than anyone can bear. So I will quit on the brown notes of this last paragraph.

P. S. I haven't seen a sparrow for awhile. Too much indoor living and indoor writing. Now it is time for you and me to go outdoors and let spring free us from ourselves.

24. Afterword

A book like this may give the impression of reproducing the actual prayer life of the author. Perhaps it does, but only indirectly. For the writer, the poet, enters into himself (often painfully) to create some order out of his confused and sometimes chaotic inner life. This is an intensely self-conscious kind of activity and as such is the very opposite of prayer which actually frees one from self-consciousness and introspection. True prayer is a liberating experience and has nothing to do with navel gazing and a heightened awareness of the self. Rather the self is "lost" in contemplation of the other, in wonder at what is not itself.

These poems and meditations, then, although they grew out of moments of heightened awareness, do not really represent or reproduce my own prayer experience. For one's prayer life is in a sense inexpressible and can at most be hinted at through symbols that merely approximate the real experience. Because the use of symbols is a conscious and reflective act, the real prayer experience is lost. For when someone prays, he does not watch himself praying or analyze what is happening or think how he is going to communicate his experience to others. He merely surrenders his deepest self to the Spirit and loses himself in God.

It is only after prayer or in periods of darkness that the mind tries to remember symbolically how it was and what it was that happened. Many of these poems and meditations, for example, are exercises of the creative process that goes on between the real experiences of God. They are like doodles that the artist makes or songs that the singer sings while he is waiting for the muse or for the Spirit to free him from self-conscious activity and enable him to be lost again in contemplation of something or someone other than himself. They are meant to fill in the time with man-made meaning until something happens and the Lord returns again.